WITHDRAWN

Pocket

MILAN & THE LAKES

TOP SIGHTS · LOCAL LIFE · MADE EASY

D1425257

In This Book

QuickStart Guide

Your keys to under-standing the city – we help you decide what to do and how to do it

Need to Know
Tips for a smooth trip

Neighbourhoods
What's where

Explore city

The best things to see and do, neighbourhood by neighbourhood

Top Sights
Make the most of your visit

Local Life
The insider's city

The Best of city

The city's highlights in handy lists to help you plan

Best Walks
See the city on foot

Milan & The Lakes' Best...
The best experiences

Survival Guide

Tips and tricks for a seamless, hassle-free city experience

Getting Around
Travel like a local

Essential Information
Including where to stay

Our selection of the city's best places to eat, drink and experience:

◎ **Sights**

✖ **Eating**

◯ **Drinking**

✪ **Entertainment**

🔒 **Shopping**

These symbols give you the vital information for each listing:

☏	Telephone Numbers	👪	Family-Friendly
⊘	Opening Hours	🐾	Pet-Friendly
P	Parking	🚌	Bus
⊗	Nonsmoking	⛴	Ferry
@	Internet Access	M	Metro
🛜	Wi-Fi Access	S	Subway
🍴	Vegetarian Selection	⊖	London Tube
📖	English-Language Menu	🚋	Tram
		🚆	Train

Find each listing quickly on maps for each neighbourhood:

Bar Hemingway

16 ◯ Map p233, B2

Legend has it that Hemi self, wielding a machine rate this timber-pan ered bar during showpiece is a en by Papa ar town. Dress s.com; Hôtel Rit ⊘6.30pm-2a

Lonely Planet's Milan & The Lakes

Lonely Planet Pocket Guides are designed to get you straight to the heart of the city.

Inside you'll find all the must-see sights, plus tips to make your visit to each one really memorable. We've split the city into easy-to-navigate neighbourhoods and provided clear maps so you'll find your way around with ease. Our expert authors have searched out the best of the city: walks, food, nightlife and shopping, to name a few. Because you want to explore, our 'Local Life' pages will take you to some of the most exciting areas to experience the real Milan & The Lakes.

And of course you'll find all the practical tips you need for a smooth trip: itineraries for short visits, how to get around, and how much to tip the guy who serves you a drink at the end of a long day's exploration.

It's your guarantee of a really great experience.

Our Promise

You can trust our travel information because Lonely Planet authors visit the places we write about, each and every edition. We never accept freebies for positive coverage, so you can rely on us to tell it like it is.

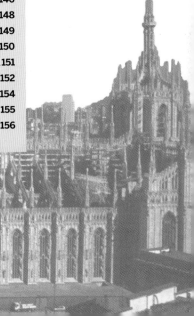

QuickStart Guide

Welcome to Milan & the Lakes

Milan is Italy's city of the future, a fast-paced metropolis where creativity is big business, looking good is compulsory and after-work drinks *(aperitivi)* are an art form. It's also a city with ancient roots and extraordinary treasures that you'll get to experience without the usual queues of tourists. Then, at the weekend, join the urban exodus to the elegant towns and tiered gardens of the Italian lakes.

Duomo (p26)
RICHARD I'ANSON/GETTY IMAGES ©

Milan & the Lakes
Top Sights

Duomo (p26)

With its ageless marble facade and countless pinnacles and spires piercing the sky, Milan's splendid Gothic cathedral is a veritable outdoor sculpture museum

Museo del Novecento (p32)

Milan's stunning collection of 20th-century art finally has the home it deserves: Italo Rota's remodelled Arengario with its floor-to-ceiling windows overlooking the Duomo.

Teatro alla Scala (p30)

Six storeys of boxes and galleries are bedecked in gilt and lined in crimson – and (for evening performances at least) audiences are similarly turned out. If you miss out on a show, visit the museum.

Museo Poldi-Pezzoli (p46)

Pezzoli's historically themed apartments, decorated with his priceless collection of Renaissance paintings and artefacts, offer a unique preserved-in-amber insight into the heyday of 19th-century patronage.

Museo Nazionale della Scienza e Tecnologia (p94)

The Leonardo da Vinci Museum of Science and Technology is one of the finest museums in Italy with interactive exhibits and models of da Vinci's radical machines.

Bellagio (p128)

Wander Bellagio's zigzagging streets and rhododendron-filled gardens, then sit lakeside and while away the afternoon with a bottle of Mamete Prevostini Opera Bianco. Surely life doesn't get any better?

Triennale di Milano (p78)

Milan's creative reputation is inextricably linked to the fashion and design industries. Founded in 1933 this vast exhibition space continues to champion the work of Italy's brightest architects and designers.

Basilica di Santa Maria delle Grazie (p92)

Saved from WWII bombs by a bank of sandbags, da Vinci's *Il Cenacolo* (The Last Supper), on the refectory wall of Santa Maria delle Grazie, is one of the world's iconic images.

Pinacoteca di Brera
(p60)

Founded in the 18th century alongside Italy's most prestigious art academy, the Pinacoteca houses the teaching aids of the day: a priceless collection of Old Master paintings including the likes of Titian, Tintoretto, Veronese and the Bellini brothers.

Isole Borromeo
(p118)

Designed so the island would have the appearance of a vessel, with the villa at its prow and the gardens dripping down 10 tiered terraces at the rear, the palace of Isola Bella and the gardens of Isola Madre are the nobility's fantasy land.

Castello Sforzesco
(p76)

The long-time seat and residence of the Dukes of Milan, the Sforza castle is one of the biggest citadels in Europe with walls that once ran 3.5km and 12 sturdy bastions. It now houses the city's civic museums.

Milan & the Lakes
Local Life

Insider tips to help you find the real city

It's true the Milanese don't always have time to play nice for visitors – they're simply too busy redesigning the world. But if you're prepared to jump in, they'll happily share their intoxicating round of pursuits, be that precision shopping, browsing contemporary galleries or loading up a plate with local delicacies while downing an expertly mixed Negroni beside Navigli's sleepy canals.

Shop Like a Local (p48)

▶ Fashion boutiques
▶ Historical palazzi

With more than 500 luxury fashion marques crammed into 6000 sq metres of cobbled laneways, the Quadrilatero d'Oro is high-fashion theatre at its best. Names like Armani, Bulgari and D&G are known the world over, but the Quad is also home to historical ateliers and heritage guilds.

Life in Parco Sempione (p80)

▶ Alfresco cafes
▶ Frisbee matches

With its winding paths, pretty ponds and baize-like lawns, much-loved Parco Sempione provides locals with a leafy oasis in the heart of Milan. Join joggers, frisbee players, canoodling couples and office workers in its alfresco cafes and admire its collection of architectural conversation pieces.

Life on the Canals (p104)

▶ Traditional trattorie
▶ Aperitivo bars

Milan was once defined by its network of canals, which fell into disuse in the 20th century. Today the banks of the Naviglio Grande and Naviglio Pavese are lined with some of the city's best trattorie, artists' workshops, bars and nightclubs. At weekends locals flock here for sunny strolls and weekend markets.

Zona Tortona (p114)

▶ Designer studios
▶ Parco Solari swimming pool

Across Graffitti Bridge, behind the railway tracks of Porta Genova, the Zona Tortona was once a tangle of working-class tenements and factories. Now flush with shopkeepers, ateliers and fashion HQ's this is the place to rub shoulders with Milan's up-and-coming designers.

Nightlife in Navigli (p110)

Dining along Naviglio Grande (p105)

Other great places to experience the city like a local:

Idroscalo (p40)

Chinatown (p87)

Fondazione Prada (p108)

Aperitivo at Pandenus (p53)

San Siro Stadium (p98)

Gelateria Marghera (p99)

Pescheria da Claudio (p67)

Cannobio's lakeside market (p117)

Milan & the Lakes
Day Planner

Day One

If you only have one day in Milan focus on the major sites. Rise early and grab a coffee and custard-filled brioche at **Princi** (p67), before climbing the stairs to the roof of the **Duomo** (p26) for a rare bird's-eye view of the city. Then head into the **Museo del Novecento** (p32) for a blast of 20th-century art. On the 3rd floor stop for lunch at **Giacomo Arengario** (p33) and nab a table on the terrace overlooking the Duomo's extravagant spires.

Then stroll down the **Galleria Vittorio Emanuele II** (p34), window shop at the original Prada shop, then pass **La Scala** (p30) on your way to the red-brick bulwark of the **Castello** (p76). Nip round the Ducal apartments admiring frescoes and Michelangelo's moving *Rondanini Pietà*, his last work. Break for *aperitivo* in the park, on the terrace of **Bar Bianco** (p81).

Then, with pre-booked tickets in hand, head over for an evening tour of **Il Cenacolo** (p93) in the dimly lit refectory, before heading back to Piazza di Duomo for a Michelin-starred dinner at **Trussardi alla Scala** (p36).

Day Two

Coffee at historical **Cova** (p48) in the Quad should start your second day. Then wander the high-fashion lanes marvelling at the window displays and buying small treats such as jewel-coloured gloves from **Sermoneta** (p57) or striped silk socks from **Gallo** (p57). End up on Via Manzoni at the aristocratic home of **Gian Giacomo Poldi Pezzoli** (p46) and tour the interiors, holding back gasps at the lavish decor and priceless Renaissance artworks.

Lunch in the internal courtyard of the Bagatti Valsecchi mansion at **Il Salumaio** (p49).Then wander over to Via Mozart and duck behind the high walls of modernist **Villa Necchi Campiglio** (p35) to see how modern-day aristocrats, Nedc and Gigina Necchi, lived in the 1930s. The house is full of delightful quotidian details their monogrammed hairbrushes and luggage, kitchen cupboards full of crockery, and silk evening frocks hanging at the ready for evenings at the La Scala.

Hop on tram 9 and whizz down to Navigli (p104) to join the throng of Milanese gathering for sunset *aperitivo*. Eat at Slow Food–recommended **Le Vigne** (p109) before taking heading to **La Salumeria della Musica** (p112) for some live music.

hort on time?

e've arranged Day Planner's must-sees into these day-by-day itineraries to make
ire you see the very best of the city in the time you have available.

ay Three

☀ Wherever you're based, make a
pilgrimage to **Gattullo** (p110) or
iffi Pasticceria (p99) to breakfast on
eam-filled sfogliatella pastries and wild
rawberry tarts. Then head west for a long
orning exploring the **Museo Nazionale
ella Scienza e della Tecnologia** (p94),
iking a peek at Bramante's serene clois-
rs at the Università del Sacro Cuore and
hipping around the many medieval treas-
res at the **Basilica di Sant'Ambrogio**
)97), on your way. Between Leonardo's
iodel machines and 17th-century
enetian astrolabes, take a break at **Bar
lagenta** (p99).

☀ After a quick panino, take a con-
templative hour with Bernardino
uini's fresco cycle at the **Chiesa di San
laurizio** (p97). See who can spot the
iost tortured saint or head to the back
f the convent to enjoy the wonderful
loah's Ark with its gang of animals.
rom there, head up to **Parco Sempi-
ne** (p80). If it's sunny climb the **Torre
ranca** (p81) for 360-degree views,
hen head into the Triennale di Milano for
peritivo with the design crowd.

☾ Finish the day in Brera's pretty
cobbled laneways with a Milanese
east at **Ristorante Solferino** (p66) or the
harming **Latteria di San Marco** (p66).

Day Four

☀ Head out of the city on the train
to Como, or Stresa on Lake Maggiore. If you head to Como, wander the
mansion-lined Passeggiata di Lino Gelpi
to **Villa Olmo** (p132) for a blockbuster
art show; if you're in Stresa, hop on the
hydrofoil to the **Isole Borromeo** (p118)
to explore one of the lavish Borromean
palaces and gardens in the bay. Lunch
on traditional lake specialities at either
Ristorante Il Vicoletto (p124) in Stresa
or **Crotto del Sergente** (p135) in Como.

☀ In the afternoon, relax – you're on
holiday! Wander the hothouses
and picnic amid tulips and camellias at
Villa Taranto (p122), or nab a sun lounge
beside the pool at the Lido di Villa Olmo.
Then take a lakeside cable car up **Monte
Mottarone** (p122) on Lake Maggiore or
to **Brunate** (p132) from Como for far-
reaching views over villages and lake.

☾ Tired and happy, take the train
back to Milan and wrap things up
with memorable cocktails, mixed with
vintage liquors, and delicious sushi aperitivo at the **Bulgari Hotel** (p67).

Need to Know

**For more information,
see Survival Guide (p157)**

Currency
Euro (€)

Language
Italian

Visas
Generally not required for stays of up to
three months.

Money
ATMs widely available. Credit cards
accepted in most restaurants and hotels.

Mobile Phones
Local SIM cards can be used in European
and Australian phones. Other phones must
be set to roaming.

Time
Central European Time (GMT plus one hour)

Plugs & Adaptors
Italy uses plugs with two or three round pins.
The electric current is 220V, 50Hz, but older
buildings may still use 125V.

Tipping
In restaurants leave a 10% tip if there is
no service charge. In bars, small change
is sufficient (€0.10 or €0.20). Tipping taxi
drivers is not common practice.

1 Before You Go

Your Daily Budget

Budget less than €100
▶ Dorm beds €15–€25
▶ Excellent markets and delis for self-caterin
▶ *Aperitivo* and all-you-can-eat buffet €8–€1

Midrange €100–€180
▶ Double room in a hotel €120–€180
▶ Two-course lunch with glass of wine in
local trattorie €25–€35

Top End more than €180
▶ Double room in four-star hotel €220–€50
▶ Dinner in Michelin-starred restaurant €150
▶ Good seats at La Scala opera €85–€210

Useful Websites

Lonely Planet (www.lonelyplanet.com/milan)
Destination information, bookings and more.

Milan City Tourism (www.turismo.comune
.milano.it) Milan's official tourism portal.

Vivimilano (www.vivimilano.it) Restaurant
and cultural listings from *Corriere della Sera*

Milano2Night (http://milano.tonight.eu)
Latest bar listings and *aperitivo* hot spots.

Advance Planning

Three months before Book tickets for *Il Cenacolo* and La Scala; if visiting during Fashion
Week or Salone del Mobile, book your hotel.

One month before Book tables at top restaurants; rustle up football tickets; arrange
appointments for bespoke tailoring.

One week before Get on the guest list at
Plastic's London Loves; see www.vivimilan
.it for restaurant and gallery openings;
arrange dry cleaning (scruffy won't do).

2 Arriving in Milan

ost visitors to Milan and the Lakes will
rive via one of the international airports,
alpensa or Linate, or through the main train
ation, Stazione Centrale. Public transport
nd private taxis are available from each hub.
ne Malpensa Express train links the main
rport to Stazione Centrale and Cadorna.

Milan Malpensa

Destination	Best Transport
Piazza di Duomo	Malpensa Express to Stazione Centrale, MM3 metro line to Duomo
Parco Sempione	Malpensa Express to Cadorna
Navigli	Malpensa Express to Cadorna, MM2 metro line to Porta Genova
Lake Maggiore	Malpensa Express to Stazione Centrale, connecting train to Stresa
Lake Como	Malpensa Express to Cadorna, connecting train to Como Nord Lago (Stazione FNM)

Milan Linate

Destination	Best Transport
Piazza di Duomo	ATM city bus to Piazza San Babila, MM1 metro line to Duomo
Quadrilatero d'Oro	ATM city bus or taxi to Piazza San Babila
Navigli	ATM city bus to Piazza Risorgimento, tram 9 to Porta Genova
Lake Maggiore	Taxi or city bus to Stazione Centrale, connecting train to Stresa

3 Getting Around

Milan's public transport system is affordable
and efficient. Most visitors will get every-
where they need to go by walking, taking the
metro, or hopping on a tram. The unlimited
one-/two-day tickets for bus, tram and
metro represent the best value for money.

M Metro

Milan's metro consists of three main
underground lines (red MM1, green MM2,
yellow MM3) and the blue suburban line the
Passante Ferroviario, and runs from 6am to
midnight. A ticket costs €1.50 and is valid for
one metro ride or up to 90 minutes' travel
on ATM buses and trams. An unlimited one-/
two-day ticket for bus, tram and metro costs
€4.50/8.25. Tickets are sold at metro stations, tobacconists and newspaper stands.
Tickets must be validated (time stamped) on
buses and trams.

Tram

Milan's trams range from beloved orange,
early-20th-century rattling cars to modern
lightrail vehicles, crisscrossing and circling
the city. They run similar hours to the metro
and tickets must be prepurchased and
validated when boarding. Important tram
lines to remember are 1, 2, 3 (all running
to the Duomo), 9 (circling the city to Porta
Genova), and 29 and 30 (serving the middle
ring road and Porta Venezia).

Taxi

Taxis are only available at designated taxi
ranks; you cannot flag them down. Alternatively, phone 02 40 40, 02 69 69 or 02 85
85 and be aware that meters are on from the
receipt of call, not from pick up. The average
short city ride costs €10.

Milan's
Neighbourhoods

Parco Sempione & Porta Garibaldi (p72)

Watched by the iconic castle and the Triennale di Milano, these areas boast stunning architecture and nightlife.

◉ Top Sights

Castello Sforzesco

Triennale di Milano

Corso Magenta & Sant'Ambrogio (p90)

One of Milan's most chic neighbourhoods, Corso Magenta is where you'll find *Il Cenacolo* and the Basilica di Sant'Ambrogio.

◉ Top Sights

Basilica di Santa Maria delle Grazie

Museo Nazionale della Scienza e Tecnologia

Navigli & Porta Romana (p102)

The south of the city is bisected by canals and is where the hipper kids come to shop and party.

Triennale di Milano ◉

Castello ◉
Sforzesco

Basilica di
Santa Maria ◉
delle Grazie

Teatro ◉
alla Scala

Duomo

◉ Museo Nazionale
della Scienza e
della Tecnologia

Lago Maggiore (p116)
Lago di Como (p126)
👁 **Top Sights**
Isole Borromeo

Bellagio

Quadrilatero d'Oro & Giardini Pubblici (p42)
Milan's luxury enclave combines cobbled streets with high-fashion theatre, flanked by a pretty pleasure garden.

👁 **Top Sights**
Museo Poldi-Pezzoli

Brera (p58)
A study in boho raffishness, Brera is home to Italy's most prestigious art school, while galleries and students abound.

👁 **Top Sights**
Pinacoteca di Brera

Duomo & San Babila (p22)
The historical centre is dominated by the twin temples of the Duomo and the Galleria Vittorio Emanuele II.

👁 **Top Sights**
Duomo

Teatro alla Scala

Museo del Novecento

Explore
Milan & the Lakes

Worth a Trip

Galleria Vittorio Emanuele II (p34)
PAOLO CORDELLI/GETTY IMAGES ©

Explore

Duomo
& San Babila

Milan's centre is conveniently compact. The splendid cathedral sits in a vast piazza thronged with tourists and touts. From here, choose God or Mammon, art or music, or take in all four at the Galleria Vittorio Emanuele II, La Scala opera house and the galleries of Palazzo Reale. Further west, the city's interior design showrooms cluster around Piazza San Babila, amid grand Novecento and Liberty buildings.

The Sights in a Day

 Head to the **Duomo** (p26) early for sublime early-morning light through the stained-glass windows and stroll around the gargoyled parapets. If it is a sunny day you may even be able to spy the Alps over the rooftops. Then drop into elegant **Giacomo Caffè** (p37) for a creamy *marocchino* coffee and brioche under the arches of the **Palazzo Reale** (p34).

For lunch sample Milan's famous saffron risotto at **Peck Italian Bar** (p37), before immersing yourself in Milan's modernist showcase, the **Museo del Novecento** (p32). Meander up the spiral staircase (a homage to the Guggenheim) admiring dynamic canvases by Umberto Boccioni and moving terracotta sculptures by Arturo Martini. End with a cocktail in the museum's 3rd-floor **Giacomo Arengario** (p33) with peerless views over the Duomo's spires. It will then be time to join the throngs window-shopping in the **Galleria Vittorio Emanuele II** (p34).

Finish the day with cocktails at the uncompromisingly cool **Straf Bar** (p37) and consider checking out what's on at the **Piccolo Teatro** (p38). For **Teatro alla Scala** (p30), opera and ballet fans will have needed to plan ahead for a night at the theatre.

 Top Sights

Duomo (p26)

Museo del Novecento (p32)

Teatro alla Scala (p30)

 Best of Milan

History
Duomo (p26)

Biblioteca e Pinacoteca Ambrosiana (p34)

Architecture
Duomo (p26)

Villa Necchi Campiglio (p35)

Chiesa di Santa Maria (p34)

Eating
Ristorante da Giacomo (p36)

Trattoria da Pino (p36)

Culture
Teatro alla Scala (p30)

Piccolo Teatro (p38)

Getting There

M Metro Take the red line (MM1) for Duomo. Continue one stop further to exit at Piazza San Babila.

🚊 Tram Numerous trams stop at Piazza Duomo; the most useful are trams 1, 2 and 3 serving the north and south of the city.

E Palestro
Galleria d'Arte Moderna

F

G

H

M Palestro

Via Poerio

Via Castel Morrone

Marina

S Primo

Via Carlo Goldoni

Viale Luigi Majno

Via Mozart

⊙5
Villa Necchi Campiglio

8 ✕ 17

Piazza del Tricolore

Piazza Risorgimento

Corso Monforte

Corso Indipendenza

SAN BABILA

Via Pietro Mascagni

Via Macedonio Melloni

Via Pasquale Sottocorno

23 🔒

Via Cerva

Viale Premuda

Viale Bianca Maria

✕
7

Via Archimede

Via Fiamma

Via Marcona

Via Fratelli Bronzetti

9 ✕

Via Filippo Corridoni

Via C Battisti

Piazza Cinque Giornate

Corso di Porta Vittoria

Corso XXII Marzo

Via Carlo Freguglia

Via Bezzecca

Via Pace

Largo Marinai d'Italia

For reviews see	
⊙ Top Sights	p26
⊙ Sights	p34
✕ Eating	p36
🍷 Drinking	p37
★ Entertainment	p38
🔒 Shopping	p38

🧭N 0 ——————— 500 m
0 ——————— 0.25 miles

Top Sights
Duomo

A vision in pink Candoglia marble, Milan's cathedral aptly reflects the city's creative brio and ambition. Begun by Gian Galeazzo Visconti in 1387, its design was originally considered unfeasible. Canals had to be dug to transport the vast quantities of marble to the city centre and new technologies were invented to cater for the never-before-attempted scale. Now its pearly-white facade rises like the filigree of a fairytale tiara, and wows the crowds with its extravagant details.

 Map p24, C3

www.duomomilano.it

Piazza del Duomo

crypt free; roof stairs/lift €7/12; treasury €2

⊙terraces 9am-9pm, treasury 9.30am-5pm Mon-Sat

Ⓜ Duomo

Interior, Duomo

Don't Miss

The Exterior

During his stint as King of Italy, Napoleon offered to fund the Duomo's completion in 1805. The architect piled on the neo-Gothic details – a homage to the original design that displayed a prescient use of fashion logic, ie everything old is new again. The organic ferment of petrified pinnacles, cusps, buttresses, rampant arches and over 3000 statues are almost all products of the 19th century.

Roof Terraces & Lantern

Climb to the roof terraces from where you are within touching distance of the elaborate 135 spires and their forest of flying buttresses. In the centre of the roof rises the 15th-century octagonal lantern and spire, on top of which is the golden Madonnina (erected in 1774). For centuries she was the highest point in the city (108.5m) until the Pirelli skyscraper outdid her in 1958.

The Interior

Initially designed so Milan's then-population of around 40,000 could fit within, the cathedral's elegant, hysterical and sublimely spiritual architecture can even transport 21st-century types back to a medieval mindset. Inside, once your eyes have adjusted to the subdued light and surreal proportions (there are five grandiose naves supported by 52 columns), stare up, and up, to the largest stained-glass windows in all of Christendom.

The Floors

Before you wander among the cathedral's many treasures, look down at your feet and marvel at the design of the polychrome marble floors that sweep across 12,000 sq metres. The design was conceived by Pellegrino Tibaldi and took 400 years to complete. The pink and white blocks

☑ Top Tips

▶ Hours for the treasury, crypt, baptistry and roof vary so check the website for details.

▶ The €13 combination ticket for the roof terraces, baptistry and treasury is a good deal.

▶ It's quicker to ascend to the roof via the 165 steps rather than the tiny elevator, which attracts a long queue.

▶ From 4 November to Epiphany, the great *Quadroni di San Carlo* paintings depicting scenes from the life of Saint Charles are displayed down the nave.

✕ Take a Break

For coffee, nip into Giacomo Caffè (p37) in the courtyard of Palazzo Reale. But to admire some of the 3500 sculptures on the Duomo's soaring spires, book at table at Giacomo Arengario (p33) on the 3rd floor of Museo del Novecento.

of Candoglia marble came from the cathedral's own quarries at Mergozzo (bequeathed in perpetuity by Gian Galeazzo), and are inset with black marble from Varenna and red marble from Arzo.

The Sun Dial

On the floor by the main entrance you may notice a brass strip lined with signs of the zodiac. This is, in fact, an 18th-century sun dial, installed by astronomers from the Accademia di Brera in 1768. A hole in the vault of the south aisle casts a ray of sunlight at various points along its length (depending on the season) at astronomical noon. The device was so precise that all the city's clocks were set by it until the 19th century.

St Bartholomew

One of the more unusual statues is the 1562 figure of St Bartholomew by Marco d'Agrate, a student of Leonardo da Vinci. It depicts St Bartholomew post-torture with his skin flayed from his flesh and cast about his neck like a cape. For 16th century anatomists he was a favourite subject, enabling sculptors to show off their anatomical knowledge as well as their technique.

The Transept

Bisecting the nave, the transept is especially rich in works of art. At either end there is an altar decorated with polychrome marbles, the most elaborate being the *Altar to the Virgin of the Tree* on the north side. In front of this stands the monumental, 5m-high

Milan Duomo

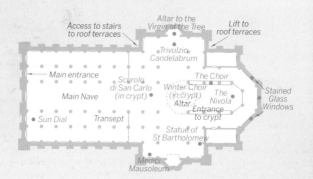

Trivulzio candelabrum, a masterpiece of medieval bronze work, its seven branches inset with precious stones.

The Choir

Completed in 1614, the sculpted choir stalls were designed by Pellegrino Tibaldi and carved by Paolo de'Gazzi, Virgilio del Conte and the Taurini brothers. The three tiers represent the life of Milanese bishops Anatalone and Galdino at the base, the martyred saints in the centre and the life of St Ambrose above.

The Nivola

High up in the apse, a red light signifies the the cathedral's most precious relic: a nail said to be from Christ's cross, stored a 16th-century wooden basket *(nivola)*. During the annual Feast of the Exaltation of the Cross (Saturday closest to 14 September), the archbishop retrieves it from the roof, and it is displayed for three days.

The Crypt

From the ambulatory that encircles the choir are the stairs down to the crypt or Winter Choir. Also designed by Tibaldi, this jewel-like circular chapel with its red porphyry pillars, polychrome marble floor and stucco ceiling contains a casket holding the relics of various saints and martyrs. A wooden choir stall encircles the room.

Scurolo di San Carlo

Through a gap in the crypt's choir stalls, a dark corridor heads to the depths of the cathedral and a memo-

RICHARD I'ANSON/GETTY IMAGES©

Duomo rooftop

rial chapel housing the remains of the saintly Carlo Borromeo, cardinal archibishop of Milan (1564–84). They're contained in a fabulous rock crystal casket atop a silver altar.

Veneranda Fabbrica del Duomo

The epic building of Milan's cathedral necessitated the creation of a 'Factory' for all operational activities and maintenance – the Fabbrica del Duomo. It oversaw the Duomo's construction from 1387 until the last gate was inaugurated in 1965. Today it continues the work of restoring and maintaining the cathedral. It's possible to visit the Fabbrica's marble quarries at Lago Mergozzo, near Lago Maggiore.

Top Sights
Teatro alla Scala

Stendhal had an attack of his very own syndrome: a fainting dizziness and confusion brought on by an excess of culture – on meeting Byron in a Marquis' box at La Scala in 1816. Modern renovations may have taken place behind the scenes (superior acoustics and bilingual libretto screens on the back of seats), but the theatre's charm remains resolutely of the 18th century. 'Opera remains the most boring thing in the world,' opined Stendhal, 'if it doesn't succeed in making us day dream about the secret sorrows that disturb the most apparently happy lives.'

Map p24, C2

02 86 07 75

www.teatroallascala.org

Via Filodrammatici 2

M Duomo

Teatro alla Scala

Don't Miss

The Theatre

Giuseppe Piermarini's grand 2800-seat theatre was inaugurated in 1778 with Antonio Salieri's *Europa Riconosciuta* (Europe Revealed). It replaced the previous theatre, which burnt down in a fire after a carnival gala. Costs were covered by the sale of *palchi* (private boxes) of which there are six gilt bedecked tiers with plush crimson lining. When rehearsals are not in session you can stand in boxes 13, 15 and 18 for a glimpse of the jewel-like interior.

The Loggione

Above the private boxes, two *loggione* (galleries) allow the less well-off to peek over the heads of Milanese plutocrats at one of the largest stages in Italy. Occupants of these seats, the *loggionisti,* are the opera's fiercest critics, famously booing tenor Roberto Alagna off stage in 2006, who was hurriedly replaced by understudy Antonello Palombi in his jeans and T-shirt to quieten them.

Museo Teatrale alla Scala

In the theatre's **museum** (☎ 02 8879 7473; Largo Ghiringhelli 1, Piazza della Scala; admission €6; ⊙ 9am-12.30pm, 1.30-5.30pm), portraits, harlequin costumes and a spinet inscribed with the command 'Inexpert hand, touch me not!' hint at centuries of Milanese musical drama, both on and off stage. The museum's **Livia Simoni Library** beckons buffs who want more.

Ansaldo Workshops

To glimpse the inner workings of La Scala visit the **workshops** (Map p24, A5; www.teatroallascala.org; Via Bergognone 34; per person €5), where the stage sets are crafted by more than 150 carpenters, blacksmiths and sculptors, and where some 800 to 1000 new costumes are handmade each season.

☑ **Top Tips**

▶ Both the ballet and opera season begin on 7 December, the Feast of Sant'Ambrogio.

▶ If you have your heart set on attending an opera, book online at least a month in advance.

▶ Dress to impress: this is a fashion town and a night at La Scala is still a grand occasion.

▶ Tour the Ansaldo Workshops (Tuesday and Thursday) to see the craft behind the shows.

✗ **Take a Break**

For a glass of bubbly or a light lunch, you won't find a more stylish venue than the courtyard of **Cafe Trussardi** (☎ 02 8068 8295; www.trussardiallascala.it; Piazza della Scala 5; ⊙ 7.30am-11pm Mon-Fri, 9am-11pm Sat; Ⓜ Duomo).

Otherwise go all-out at that other Milanese institution, Il Marchesino (p37), where Gualtiero Marchesi, one of Italy's most revered chefs, presides over La Scala's kitchen.

Top Sights
Museo del Novecento

Overlooking the Piazza del Duomo, with fabulous views of the cathedral, is Mussolini's Arengario, from where he would harangue huge crowds in the glory days of his regime. Now it houses Milan's museum of 20th-century art. Built around a futuristic spiral ramp (an ode to the Guggenheim), the lower floors are cramped, but the heady collection, which includes the likes of Boccioni, Campigli, De Chirico and Marinetti, more than distracts.

Map p24, C4

www.museodel
novecento.org

Via Guglielmo Marconi 1

adult/reduced €5/3

9.30am-7.30pm Tue-Sun, 2.30-7.30pm Mon

M Duomo

Interior, Museo del Novecento

Don't Miss

Palazzo dell'Arengario

The austere Arengario Palace consists of two symmetrical buildings each with a three-tier arcaded facade. It was built in the 1950s by starchitects Piero Portaluppi, Giovanni Muzio, Pier Giulio Magristretti and Enrico Griffini, and is decorated with bas reliefs by Milanese sculptor Arturo Martini, whose work now features in the museum's collection. The name *arengario* comes from the building's original function as the government seat during the Fascist period, when officials would *arringa* (harangue) the local populous from the building's balcony.

The Collection

The museum's permanent collection is an ode to 20th-century modern art, with a particular focus on Milanese talent. Chronological rooms take you from Volpedo's powerful neo-impressionist painting of striking workers, *Il Quarto Stato* (The Fourth Estate), through the dynamic work of Futurist greats such as Umberto Boccioni, Carlo Carrà, Gino Severini and Giacomo Balla, and on to Abstractism, Surrealism, Spatialism and Arte Povera. The collection provides a fascinating social commentary on Italy's trajectory through two world wars and into the technological era.

Giacomo Arengario

The other highlight of the museum is this 3rd-floor **bistro** (📞02 7209 3814; www.giacomoarengario. com; Via Guglielmo Marconi 1; meals €25-40; ⏰noon-midnight) overlooking the Duomo, where artful rooms are decorated in a luxe Art Deco style. Top-notch bistro fare includes fish platters, truffles and game, which are served by jacketed waiters. During the day, gaze out at the Duomo's spires and at night enjoy the jewel-like colours of the stained-glass windows.

☑ Top Tips

▶ Consider a guided tour, available in Italian, English and French.

▶ The museum's 3rd-floor restaurants offer an unparalleled view of the Duomo's spires and is run by the excellent people from Da Giacomo (p36).

▶ The most iconic painting in the collection is Giuseppe Pellizza da Volpedo's *The Fourth Estate*, a scene of striking workers that embodies the idea of 'mass movement'.

▶ The Arengario is linked to the Palazzo Reale (p34) by a suspended footbridge.

✗ Take a Break

Book ahead for lunch at the museum's 3rd-floor Giacomo Arengario bistro (left) to make sure you snag a seat on the terrace.

In the evening cross the piazza for drinks among the beautiful people at Straf Bar (p37).

Sights

Galleria Vittorio Emanuele II
SHOPPING ARCADE

1 ⊙ Map p24, C3

So much more than a shopping arcade, this neoclassical gallery is a soaring iron-and-glass structure known locally as *il salotto bueno* – the city's fine drawing room. Shaped like a crucifix, it also marks the *passeggiata* (promenade) route from Piazza del Duomo to Piazza di Marino and the doors of La Scala. (Piazza del Duomo; Ⓜ Duomo)

Palazzo Reale
MUSEUM, PALACE

2 ⊙ Map p24, C4

Empress Maria Theresa's favourite architect Giuseppe Piermarini gave this town hall and Visconti palace a neoclassical overhaul in the late 18th century. Its elegant interiors were all but destroyed by WWII bombs; the **Sala delle Cariatidi** remains unrenovated as a reminder of war's indiscriminate destruction. In other rooms, blockbuster shows wow the crowds with artists as diverse as Titian, Francis Bacon and Dario Fo. (www.comune.milano.it/palazzoreale; Piazza del Duomo 12; exhibitions €5-12, Museo della Reggia free; ⊙ exhibitions 2.30-7.30pm Mon, 9.30am-7.30pm Tue, Wed, Fri & Sun, 9.30am-10.30pm Thu & Sat, Museo 9.30am-5.30pm Tue-Sun; Ⓜ Duomo)

Biblioteca e Pinacoteca Ambrosiana
LIBRARY, ART GALLERY

3 ⊙ Map p24, B4

The Biblioteca Ambrosiana, built in 1609 by Cardinal Borromeo, was Europe's first public library and houses more than 75,000 volumes including Leonardo da Vinci's priceless *Codex Atlanticus*. Later an art gallery, the **Pinacoteca**, was added to exhibit Italian paintings from the 14th to the 20th century, most famously Caravaggio's *Canestra di Frutta* (Basket of Fruit), which launched his career and Italy's ultrarealist traditions. (✆02 80 69 21; www.ambrosiana.it; Piazza Pio XI 2; adult/reduced €15/10; ⊙10am-6pm Tue-Sun; Ⓜ Duomo)

Chiesa di Santa Maria Presso di San Satiro
CHURCH

4 ⊙ Map p24, B4

Here's an escape from the Zara/Benetton maelstrom. Ludovico Sforza saw potential in this little church built on top of the mausoleum of martyr San Satiro, and asked architect Donato Bramante to refurbish it in 1482. His ambition wasn't dampened by the project's scale: a trompe-l'oeil coffered niche on the apse makes the backdrop to the altar mimic the Pantheon in Rome. (Via Speronari 3; admission free; ⊙7.30-11.30am Mon-Fri, 3.30-6.30pm Sat; Ⓜ Duomo)

Galleria Vittorio Emanuele II

Villa Necchi Campiglio VILLA

5 ⊚ Map p24, E2

Set in a beautiful garden with a swimming pool, tennis court and tall magnolia trees, this 1932 Piero Portaluppi–designed house is a symbol of Milan's wealth and modernist imaginings. The superbly refurbished interiors are redolent of the Necchi sisters' privileged lifestyles, with a profusion of domestic detail, while the walls are hung with fabulous 20th-century Italian paintings. (☎02 7634 0121; www .casemuseo.it; Via Mozart 14; adult/reduced €8/4; ☺10am-6pm Wed-Sun; Ⓜ San Babila)

Chiesa di San Bernardino alle Ossa CHURCH, OSSUARY

6 ⊚ Map p24, D4

This church dates from the 13th century, when its ossuary was used to bury plague victims from nearby San Barnaba hospital. It was rebuilt in rococo style in 1679, after it collapsed beneath the fallen belltower of adjacent Santo Stefano. The walls of the new ossuary, with its frescoed vault, *Triumph of Souls Among Flying Angels,* are now lined with a macabre flourish in human bones, finished with the skulls of condemned prisoners. (☎02 855 63 04; Via Carlo Giuseppe Merlo 4; admission free; ☺7.30am-noon & 1-6pm Mon-Fri, 7.30am-noon Sat, 9am-noon Sun; 🚊12, 15, 23, 27)

Eating

Ristorante da Giacomo
SEAFOOD €€

 7

This classy Tuscan restaurant, with its sage-green panelling and embossed wallpaper, serves an accomplished menu focusing on fish and shellfish. Start with a complimentary sardine and caper pizza and follow with the crab linguine and langoustine with cherry tomatoes. Truffles and porcini also feature in season. (☑02 7602 3313; www.giacomomilano.com; Via Pasquale Sottocorno 6; meals €30-40; 🚋9, 23)

Cantina di Manuela
ENOTECA €€

 8

A wine bar with an impressive kitchen focusing on cured meats, succulent Fiorentina steaks and cutlets. Locals

also come after work to pick up a bottle of wine or share a generous platter of goat's cheese, honey and *mostarda* over a glass while their kids munch on bread and draw. (☑02 7631 8892; www.lacantinadimanuela.it; Via Poerio 3; meals €25-35; ⏱11am-1.30am Mon-Sat; 🚋9, 23)

Trattoria da Pino
MILANESE €

 9

In a city full of models in Michelin-starred restaurants, working-class da Pino's offers the perfect antidote. Sit elbow-to-elbow at long cafeteria-style tables in the rust-red dining room and order up bowls of *bollito misto* (mixed boiled meats), handmade pasta and curried veal nuggets. (☑02 7600 0532; Via Cerva 14; meals €20-25; ⏱noon-3pm Mon-Sat; Ⓜ San Babila)

Trussardi alla Scala
CONTEMPORARY ITALIAN €€€

 10

Whether it's for stylish *aperitivo* at the cafe bar beneath Patrick Blanc's vertical garden, or a blow-out meal in Andrea Berton's sexy, Michelin-starred dining room, Trussardi offers some of the finest dining near the Duomo. The food also has a directness, with seasonal dishes such as roast spring lamb with potato, avocado and lime. (☑02 8068 8201; www.trussardiallascala.com; Piazza della Scala 5; meals €120; ⏱7.30am-11pm Mon-Fri, dinner Sat; ❄; Ⓜ Duomo)

Peck Italian Bar
ITALIAN €€

11 🍴 Map p24, B3

Peck's dining room lets quality produce shine with staples such as *cotoletto*, risotto and roasts done with fabulously fresh, well-sourced ingredients, if not a smidgen of contemporary flair. The room is also a picture of restraint, with wines by the glass administered by bow-tied waiters. (☎02 869 30 17; www.peck.it; Via Cesare Cantù 3; dishes €18-30; ⏱7.30am-8.30pm Mon-Sat; ❄; MDuomo)

Luini
PASTICCERIA €

12 🍴 Map p24, C3

Stockbrokers and student radicals, models and their harried hairdressers might get together here and sing 'Kumbaya', if they didn't all have their mouths full. *Panzerotti* is Milanese for yummy at this popular purveyor of pizza-dough pastries stuffed with cheeses, spinach, tomato, pesto and prosciutto. (www.luini.it; Via Santa Radegonda 16; panzerotti €2.50; ⏱10am-3pm Mon, 10am-8pm Tue-Sun; 🚻; MDuomo)

Il Marchesino
CONTEMPORARY ITALIAN €€€

13 🍴 Map p24, B2

Gualtiero Marchesi, Italy's most revered chef, presides over the dining room at La Scala. Chairs upholstered in deep crimson evoke the neighbouring concert hall. The menu is similarly traditional but infused with a creative spirit. Earthy handcut spaghetti is served with mussels and a verdant tangle of zucchini, and foie gras–scented roast pigeon is scattered with pinenuts and raisins. (☎02 7209 4338; www.ilmarchesino.it; Via Filodrammatici 2; meals €50-80, tasting menu €110; ⏱8am-1am Mon-Sat, kitchen closes 10.30pm; MDuomo)

Grom
GELATERIA €

14 🍴 Map p24, B3

The pistachio is made from nuts sourced in Sicily and the *gianduja* mixes Piemontese hazelnuts with Venezuelan chocolate. Love it or hate it, Grom is good. (☎02 8058 1041; www.grom.it; Via Santa Margherita 16; gelati €2-3; ⏱11am-11pm; ❄🚻; MDuomo)

Drinking

Giacomo Caffè
CAFE

15 🍷 Map p24, C4

Tucked beneath the arches of Palazzo Reale this literary cafe – with its secluded, upstairs reading gallery lined with book shelves and artwork – is a tranquil spot to recharge from museum browsing. The 19th-century style bar, stacked with pastries, serves perfect-every-shot coffee and elegant evening aperitifs. (Piazza Reale 12; ⏱8am-8pm; MDuomo)

Straf Bar
BAR

16 🍷 Map p24, C3

Pick of the centre's hotel bars with a busy nightly *aperitivo* scene that kicks on until pumpkin hour. The decor is along the now familiar mod-exotic lines: sombre wood/metal/stone/fibreglass played up against minimalist concrete. In summer it has a calendar of live music and the party spills out into tiny Via San Raffael. (☏ 02 8050 0715; www.straf.it; Via San Raffael 3; ⏱ 8am-midnight; Ⓜ Duomo)

Gold
BAR, RESTAURANT

17 📍 Map p24, G2

Dolce & Gabbana's shiny paean to excess will either enthral or appal depending on your mood (and perhaps who's paying). The gold-themed bar, mirror-topped tables and TV's in the toilets are worth a cocktail or two, but give the restaurant a miss as style over substance only goes so far. (☏ 02 757 77 71; www.dolcegabbana.com/gold; Via Carlo Poerio 2a; ⏱ 8am-1am Mon-Wed, to 2am Thu-Sat; 🚌 9, 23)

G-Lounge
BAR

18 📍 Map p24, C4

It's Brazilian *caipirinhas* and chill-out in this fashionable corner bar. Once the club of Milan's Gerachi fascists, this place attracts guppies (gay urban professionals) and a well-heeled Friday-night crowd. There's a small ground-floor bar, but the real action takes place in the basement after 10pm. (☏ 02 805 30 42; www.glounge.it; Via Larga 8; ⏱ 7.30am-9.30pm Mon, 7.30am-2am Tue-Sun; Ⓜ Duomo)

Entertainment

Piccolo Teatro
THEATRE

19 ⭐ Map p24, B3

This risk-taking little repertory theatre was opened in 1947 by Paolo Grassi and none other than the late, great theatre director Giorgio Strehler, and then embarked on a nationwide movement of avant-garde productions and Commedia dell'Arte revivals. Additional programming, including ballet, goes on at the larger, second sibling space over at the Piccolo Teatro Strehler (p69). (☏ 02 4241 1889; www.piccoloteatro. org; Via Rovello 2; ⏱ box office 10am-6.45pm Mon-Sat, 10am-5pm Sun; Ⓜ Cordusio)

Le Banque
LOUNGE BAR, DISCO

20 ⭐ Map p24, B3

Eschewing the usual 'less is more' Milanese philosophy, Le Banque (a former bank) goes all out with baroque decor: acres of heavy red drapery, a gold bar and two basement disco halls and LCD-lit dance floors. It attracts a young, rowdy crowd of red-carpet totty and fashionistas into the Versace look. (☏ 02 8699 6565; www.lebanque.it; Via Porrone Bassano 6; ⏱ from 7pm Tue-Sun; Ⓜ Cordusio)

Shopping

Borsalino
ACCESSORIES

21 🔒 Map p24, C3

This iconic Alessandrian milliner has worked with design greats like Achille Castiglioni, who once designed

Understand
Reinventing Milan

- -

The Rise of Mussolini
Benito Mussolini's political career began in Milan, and he swiftly moved from words to action through his paramilitary Blackshirts. His promises of strength and national unity had broad appeal, and by 1922 he was prime minister. San Siro stadium was built in 1926, combining Fascism's Rationalist modernity and Mussolini's fetish for the camper side of Imperial Rome. Other former Fascist monuments include Stazione Centrale, the Triennale, Palazzo dell'Arengario and the Armani shop on Via Manzotti.

World War II
WWII bombs devastated Milan, destroying a quarter of the city and leaving La Scala and the Palazzo Reale in ruins. At the same time, strikes by the Italian Resistance and anti-Fascist trade unions paralysed the city. Despite Italy's surrender to Allied forces in 1945, Mussolini declared a new Fascist republic, provoking a civil guerrilla war. The partisans prevailed and Mussolini was captured and executed along with his mistress, Carla Petacci. Their bodies were hung upside down in Piazzale Loreto.

Remembrance
The Cimitero Monumentale contains a memorial to the Milanese who died in Nazi concentration camps. Designed by Studio BBPR, the pure form of a cube is traced in steel and slab marble, a response of reason and light to the horror of the war years. At its centre is earth from the camp where Gianluigi Banfi, one of BBPR's four partners, died.

Modern Milan
After WWII reconstruction began and Milan soon became a powerhouse in transforming Italy's largely agrarian society into a modern industrial economy. More than nine million Italians migrated north between the 1950s and '70s, and many ended up in Milan and surrounding Lombard towns attracted by the steelworks, manufacturing and railway construction. Likewise, Milan's philosopher-architects rebuilt the damaged city, evolving concepts of form and function that have changed the way we live in the modern the world. These days 16% of Italy's population and 25% of its émigrés call Lombardy home and the region generates 20% of Italy's GDP.

a pudding-bowl bowler hat. This outlet in the galleria stocks seasonal favourites. The main showroom is at Corso Venezia 21a. (☑02 8901 5436; www.borsalino.com; Galleria Vittorio Emanuele II 92; ⏱Tue-Sat; Ⓜ Duomo)

Peck
FOOD, WINE

22 🔒 Map p24, B4

This multifloored food hall has been stocking Milanese pantries for more than a century. Its size won't overwhelm, but the range and quality of cheeses, oils, cured meats, chocolates, pastries, pasta and fresh produce will. Upstairs, the lunch bar is like something out of a Lucio Binetti music vid

Local Life
Idroscalo Idyll

Once the liquid landing strip for seaplanes, this **artificial lake** (☑02 7020 0902; www.provincia.milano.it/ idroscalo; Via Circonvallazione Idroscalo- near, Linate Airport) is now a summer playground. Concerts regularly take place here, including indie-leaning festivals, and there's swimming and water sports including wake-boarding and kite surfing. Check the website for details and a weekly calendar of events. Like Navigli, mosquitoes come to play, too – make sure you have good insect repellent. To get to Idroscalo, take bus 73 from San Babila to Linate Airport, then take the free shuttle.

from the early '80s. Don't miss the downstairs wine cellar on the way out. (☑02 802 31 61; www.peck.it; Via Spadari 9; ⏱9.15am-7.30pm Tue-Sat, 3.30-7.30pm Mon; ♿; Ⓜ Duomo)

Il Salvagente
FASHION

23 🔒 Map p24, H3

The grim basement courtyard of Il Salvagente gives scant indication of the big brand names inside. Discounted Prada, Dolce & Gabbana, Versace and Ferretti are just a few of the labels on the tightly packed racks. Payment is in cash only. (☑02 7611 0328; www.salvagentemilano.it; Via Fratelli Bronzetti 16; ⏱10am-7pm Tue-Sat, 3-7pm Mon; 🚌60, 62, 92)

Hoepli International Bookstore
BOOKSHOP

24 🔒 Map p24, C3

Italy's largest bookshop has six floors and some 500,000 titles, as well as rare antiquarian books and an English- and German-language section. Don't neglect to browse the Italian shelves, even if you don't speak the language, as local publishers are known for their beautiful cover design and innovative pictorial titles. (☑02 86 48 71; www.hoepli.it; Via Ulrico Hoepli 5; ⏱10am-7.30pm Mon-Sat; Ⓜ Duomo)

Piumelli
ACCESSORIES

25 🔒 Map p24, C3

Leather gloves come in a huge range of styles, every colour of the rainbow with a choice of luxury linings (silk, cashmere, lapin). For those with either delicate digits or mighty man-hands, they have a full range of sizes and friendly staff to advise on fit. Look out for the sales baskets when not just after basic black. (📞02 869 23 18; www .piumelli.com; Galleria Vittorio Emanuele II; ⏰10am-7pm Mon-Sat, 2-7pm Sun; Ⓜ Duomo)

Citta del Sole TOYS

26 🔒 Map p24, B3

Inspire your little Leonardo with that book on bridges designed by da Vinci or groom a mini Gae Aulenti with Bauhaus blocks. (📞02 8646 1683; www .cittadelsole.it; Via Orefici 13; ⏰10am-7.30pm Tue-Sun, 11am-7.30pm Mon; ⚥; Ⓜ Cordusio)

Rinascente DEPARTMENT STORE

27 🔒 Map p24, C3

Italy's most prestigious department store doesn't let the fashion capital down. Come for Italian diffusion lines, French lovelies and LA upstarts. The basement hides an amazing homewares department and a tax-back office for non-EU citizens, while the food market and restaurant are on the 7th floor. (📞02 8 85 21; www .rinascente.it; Piazza del Duomo; ⏰10am-midnight; Ⓜ Duomo)

CARLO BRAMBILLA 2/ALAMY ©

Peck food hall

Ē de Padova HOMEWARES, DESIGN

28 🔒 Map p24, E2

America's great modernist designer George Nelson called this shop 'one of the most beautiful in the world' and who are we to disagree? Maddalena De Padova's excellent eye has held sway here since 1965, and with six floors of great design to behold, it's a grand alternative to taking in all the showrooms if you're short of time. (📞02 77 72 01; www.depadova.it; Corso Venezia 14; ⏰3-7pm Mon, 10am-7pm Tue-Sat; Ⓜ Montenapoleone)

Explore

Quadrilatero d'Oro & Giardini Pubblici

Northeast of the Duomo, the Quadrilatero d'Oro (the Golden Quad) sings a siren song to luxury label lovers the world over. It also goes by the diminutive 'Monte Nap' after Via Monte Napoleone, which is one of its defining four streets along with Via della Spiga, Via Sant'Andrea and Via Borgospesso. To the northeast Corso Venezia borders the splendid Giardini Pubblici, a 19th-century pleasure garden.

The Sights in a Day

Start the day with a slug of the best coffee in Milan at **Il Caffè Ambrosiano** (p55). There are no seats, but you'll be rubbing elbows with local coffee connoisseurs and munching *cornetti* at the bar. Then wander south through the pretty **Giardini Pubblici** (p50). If you're *en famille* consider stopping at the **Museo Civico** (p51), Milan's oldest civic museum and Italy's most important natural history museum. Otherwise head north to the eccentric Piero Portaluppi–designed **apartment** (p50) of Antonio Boschi and Marieda di Stefano, a treasure trove of 20th-century Italian painting.

Spend the afternoon browsing the cobbled alleys of the **Quad** (p48). Lunch with models in the hushed courtyard at **Il Salumaio di Monte-napoleone** (p49), and ponder the difficult task of colour coordinating Sermoneta's rainbow-hued gloves with Aspesi's latest tobacco-coloured raincoat.

Finally elbow your way to the bar at **Pandenus** (p53) for one of the finest, and most filling, *aperitivo* buffets in town. If you don't fill up on the endless plates of bruschetta, piz-zetta, pasta and raw veg, pop round the corner to **Lon Fon** (p52).

For a local's day in Quadrilatero d'Oro, see p48.

 Top Sights

Museo Poldi-Pezzoli (p46)

 Local Life

Shop Like a Local (p48)

 Best of Milan

Art
Museo Poldi-Pezzoli (p46)

Casa Museo Boschi-di Stefano (p50)

Museo Bagatti Valsecchi (p51)

Fashion
Aspesi (p55)

G Lorenzi (p49)

Gardens
Giardini Pubblici (p50)

Drinking
Pandenus (p53)

HClub (p53)

Getting There

M Metro Use Montenapoleone (MM3, yellow line) for the Quad. For Giardini Pubblici, exit at Palestro or Porta Venezia (both on MM1, the red line). For Corso Buenos Aires and the Boschi-di Stefano museum, continue to Lima from Porta Venezia.

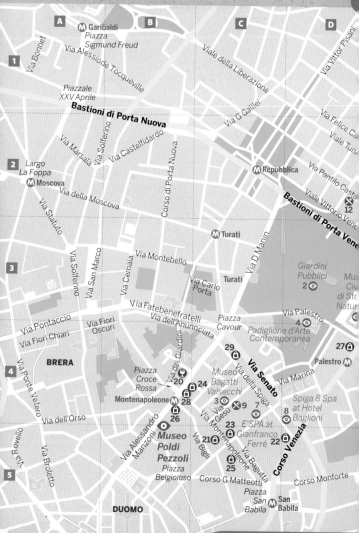

A
Ⓜ Garibaldi
Piazza
Sigmund Freud
Via Alessio de Tocqueville
Via Bonnet

B

C
Viale della Liberazione
Via G. Galilei
Ⓜ Repubblica
Via Panfilo Casta
Via Vittor Pisani

D
Via Felice Ca
Viale Tun
Via Panfilo Casta
Bastioni di Porta Vene
Ⓧ 12

Piazzale
XXV Aprile
Bastioni di Porta Nuova

Via Marsala
Via Solferino
Via Castelfidardo
Corso di Porta Nuova

Largo
La Foppa
Ⓜ Moscova
Via della Moscova

Via Statuto

Via Solferino
Via San Marco
Via Cernaia
Via Montebello
Via Carlo Porta
Via D. Manin

Ⓜ Turati

Turati

Giardini
Pubblici
2 ◉
Mus
Civ
di Sto
Natur

Via Pontaccio
Via Fiori Oscuri
Via Fiori Chiari
Via Fatebenefratelli
Via dell'Anunnciata

Piazza
Cavour
Padiglione d'Arte
Contemporanea
Via Palestro
4 ◉
27 🔒
Palestro Ⓜ

BRERA
Via Ponte Vetero

Piazza
Croce
Rossa
Via dei Giardini
20 🔒
24 🔒
28 🔒
Montenapoleone Ⓜ
26 ◉

Museo
Bagatti
Valsecchi
3 🔒 Ⓧ 9
Via Gesu
Via della Spiga
Via Senato
Via Marina
7
Spiga 8 Spa
at Hotel
Baglioni
8 ◉

29 🔒

Via Rovello
Via Broletto
Via dell'Orso

Via Alessandro Manzoni
Ⓜ
Museo
Poldi
Pezzoli
Piazza
Belgioioso
Via Bigli
Via Montenapoleone
21 🔒
23 🔒
25 🔒
E'SPA at
Gianfranco
Ferré
22 ◉
Via Bagutta
Corso Venezia

Corso G Matteotti
Piazza
San
Babila
Ⓜ San
Babila
Corso Monforte

DUOMO

E

F

G

H

Via Mauro Macchi

Via Luigi Settembrini

Via Dom Vitruvio

Via Benedetto Marcello

Via Tadino

Corso Buenos Aires

Via N Piccini

Viale Gran Sasso

1

10 ✕

13 🍴

Via Gaspare Spontini

Ⓜ Lima

Via Vitruvio

Via San Gregorio

14 🔵

Via G.B Morgagni

1 ◉
Casa Museo
Boschi-di
Stefano

Viale Abruzzi

Via Stradella

QUADRILATERO
D'ORO

Via Alessandro Tadino

Via Enrico Noe

2

17 🔵

19 🔵

Via Plinio

6 Spazio
◉ Oberdan

Via Maiocchi

Via Omboni

Ⓜ Porta
Venezia

Via Filippo Juvara

3

Viale Piave

15 🔵

Via Lambro

18 🔵

Via Melzo

Via Nino Bixio

16 🔵

Viale dei Mille

Viale Luigi Majno

Via Gustavo Modena

Via Poerio

Via Carlo Goldoni

4

Piazza del
Tricolore

Piazza
Risorgimento

SAN BABILA

Via Macedonio Melloni

Via Pasquale Sottocorno

For reviews see	
◉ Top Sights	p46
◉ Sights	p50
✕ Eating	p52
🍴 Drinking	p53
🔒 Shopping	p55

Ⓝ

0 _____ 500 m
0 _____ 0.25 miles

5

Top Sights
Museo Poldi-Pezzoli

Having inherited his vast fortune at the age of 24, Gian Giacomo Poldi Pezzoli also inherited his mother's love of art. During extensive European travels he was inspired by the 'house museum' that was later to become London's V&A. As his collection grew, Pezzoli had the idea of transforming his apartments into a series of historically themed rooms based on the great art periods of the past (the Middle Ages, Early Renaissance, Baroque and Rococo). Today these *Sala d'Artista* are works of art in themselves.

Map p44, B5

02 79 48 89

www.museopoldi
pezzoli.it

Via Alessandro Manzoni 12

adult/reduced €9/6

10am-6pm Wed-Mon

Montenapoleone

The Black Room, Museo Poldi-Pezzoli

Don't Miss

Sala d'Armi

The Armoury was the first room of Pezzoli's 'house-museum' to be completed. Its Neo-Gothic interiors were styled by La Scala set designer Filippo Peroni, but his theatrical folly was destroyed in WWII. The new room, with its tomb-like interior designed by Arnaldo Pomodoro, feels like something from a 16th-century *Raiders of the Lost Ark*.

The Grand Staircase

An impressive neo-Baroque staircase spirals up to the 1st-floor apartments around an extravagant fountain designed by Giuseppe Bertini. It's adorned with brass cherubs originally intended for the Portinari Chapel in Sant'Eustorgio (p108), but Gian Giacomo thought they'd look good in his stairwell.

Sala d'Artista

Of the original apartment only four rooms survived WWII bombs and have been refurbished in exquisite detail: the Stucco Room, in its Rococo style; the Black Room, originally clad in mahogany and ivory; the Antique Murano room, Gian Giacomo's bedroom; and the Byzantine-influenced Dante study where Pezzoli kept his prized possessions.

The Collection

As a collector, Gian Giacomo focused on his passion for arms, the decorative arts and Renaissance paintings. Wander from room to room and admire Lombard Renaissance masters Foppa, Bergognone and Luini; Tuscan and Venetian greats including Botticelli, Bellini, Mantegna and Piero della Francesca; and the beautiful *Portrait of a Young Woman* by del Pollaiolo, which is now the museum's icon. Between them you'll have to skirt around display cases of Venetian glass, 18th-century porcelain and cabinets gleaming with jewellery.

☑ Top Tips

▶ Unlike most other museums, which close on Monday, Poldi Pezzoli is closed on Tuesday.

▶ Aside from the Sala d'Artista, the museum has a unique collection of time pieces in a separate exhibit.

▶ Guided tours in a variety of languages are available for both groups and individuals. They last about an hour.

▶ The museum is part of the Casemuseocard network (p52), which offers a worthwhile discount on Milan's four 'house-museums'.

✗ Take a Break

Watch wealthy matrons stock up on sweet tarts, breads and pastries in Caffe Cova (p48), a Monte Nap institution.

Imagine you're a 19th-century aristocrat and break for lunch at Il Salumaio (p49), where bow-tied waiters bring you pancakes with porcini mushrooms and platters of *bresaolo* from the Valtellina.

Q Local Life
Shop Like a Local

For anyone interested in the fall of a frock or the cut of a jacket, a stroll around the Quadrilatero d'Oro, the world's most famous shopping district, is a must. This quaintly cobbled quadrangle of streets is full of Italy's most famous brands sporting fantastical window displays. Even if you don't have the slightest urge to sling a swag of glossy carriers over your arm, the people-watching is priceless.

1 Coffee at Cova
Coffee at **Caffé Cova** (☎02 7600 5599; www.pasticceriacova.com; Via Monte Napoleone; ☉8.30am-8pm Mon-Sat; Ⓜ️Montenapoleone) gives you a glimpse into the world of Monte Nap. Aggressively accessorised matrons crowd the neoclassical bar barking pastry orders at the aproned staff. This is the oldest cafe in Milan, opened in 1817 by Antonio Cova, a soldier of Napoleon.

2 Browsing 'Monte Nap'

Via Montenapoleone has always been synonymous with elegance and money (Napoleon's government managed loans here) and now it is the most important street of the Quad, lined with global marques like Etro, Ferragamo, Armani and Prada. Among the giants, remnants of the area's traditional past persist, as in men's grooming temple **G Lorenzi** (⏹ 02 7602 2848; www.lorenzi.it; Via Monte Napoleone 9; ⏱ Mon-Sat).

3 Lunch at Il Salumaio

When **Il Salumaio** (⏹ 02 7600 1123; www .ilsalumaiodimontenapoleone.it; Via Monte Napoleone 12; ⏱ 11am-7.30pm Mon-Fri; ✱; Ⓜ Montenapoleone) opened on Via Montenapoleone in 1957, there was an outcry from locals who thought a humble delicatessen would lower the tone of the exclusive neighbourhood. But the deli opened and quickly wowed Milanese shoppers with its extravagant window displays. It's now housed in the Bagatti Valsecchi palazzo.

4 Get Fitted for a Suit

If you ever wondered where James Bond gets his suits, head to **Brioni** (⏹ 02 7631 8718; www.brioni.com; Via Gesù 2A; ⏱ 10am-7pm Tue-Sat; Ⓜ Montenapoleone) on Via Gesù, the bespoke atelier where head tailor Mauro Stracci turns fabric into pure sex appeal. In the atelier's studio you can see the labelled paper *formes* of outfits worn by movie stars, celebrities and presidents. A cheaper off-the-peg men's shop is at No. 3, and a women's shop at No. 4.

5 Homewares on Via Manzoni

Established in Omegna in 1921, **Alessi** (⏹ 02 79 57 26; www.alessi.com; Via Manzoni 14-16; ⏱ Tue-Sun) has gone on to transform our homes with more than 22,000 crafted utensils, many of which have been designed by the world's leading architect-designers. Some of them now reside in the V&A in London and New York's MoMA, but you can just pop down to the flagship store for their most cutting-edge ranges.

6 Aperitivo on Via della Spiga

Who wouldn't love shopping on beautiful, pedestrianised Via della Spiga, once the domain of bakeries and now home to Bulgari. But if the cobbles are making those killer heels pinch, take the back door into the Hotel Baglioni for a Campari and soda in their **cafe** (⏹ 02 77 077; www.baglionihotels.com; Via Senato 5, Via della Spiga (back entrance); ⏱ 9am-1am; Ⓜ San Babila). Decked out like a 19th-century drawing room, it's a favourite haunt with ladies who lunch.

7 Visit an Aristocratic Home

For a glimpse of aristocratic life during the 18th century, wander around the Palazzo Morando Attendolo Bolognini. Housing the collections of Countess Bolognini, the apartments are also hung with the art collection of **Museo di Milano** (⏹ 02 884 6 5933; www.museo distoriacontemporanea.it; Via Sant'Andrea 6; admission free; ⏱ 2-5.30pm Tue-Sun Sep-Jul; Ⓜ San Babila), which provides a picture of the city as it was during the Napoleonic era.

Sights

Casa Museo Boschi-di Stefano HOUSE MUSEUM

1 ◉ Map p44, F2

One of Milan's best collection of 20th-century Italian paintings is crowded salon-style into a Piero Portaluppi–designed 1930s apartment that still has the appearance of the haute-bourgeois home it once was. It's a heady art hit, with Boccioni's dynamic brushstrokes propelling painting towards Futurism, the metaphysical Campigli and De Chirico, and the restless, expressionist Informels covering every inch of wall space. (📞02 2024 0568; www .fondazioneboschidistefano.it; Via Giorgio Jan 15; admission free; ⊙2-6pm Tue-Sun Sep-Jul, daily Aug; Ⓜ Lima)

Giardini Pubblici PUBLIC GARDEN

2 ◉ Map p44, D3

A life story unfolds as you follow pebble paths past bumper cars and a carousel, onward past kissing teens, a beer kiosk, baby prams, jogging paths and shady benches. Jump in, or just stop and smell the roses. For grey days the Museo Civico di Storia Naturale (p51) beckons. (Corso Venezia; ⊙6.30am-sunset; 🚻🐾; Ⓜ Palestro)

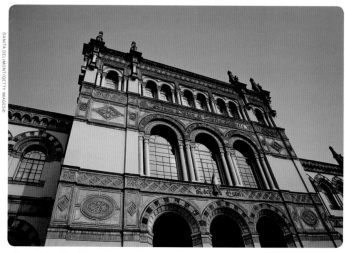

DANITA DELIMONT/GETTY IMAGES©

Museo Civico di Storia Naturale

Museo Bagatti Valsecchi

HOUSE MUSEUM

3 Map p44, C4

Though born a few centuries too late, the Bagatti Valsecchi brothers, Fausto and Giuseppe, were determined to be Renaissance men, and from 1878 to 1887 built their twin mansions as a living museum of the Quattrocento. Decorated after the style of the ducal palaces in Mantua, the apartments are full of Renaissance furnishings, ceiling friezes, tapestries and paintings. Even the period stone bath was retro-fitted discreetly for running water, a modernisation of their own era. (02 7600 6132; www.museobagattivalsecchi.org; Via Gesù 5; adult/reduced €8/4, Wed €4; 1-5.45pm Tue-Sun; Montenapoleone)

Padiglione d'Arte Contemporanea

GALLERY

4 Map p44, D3

Built in 1954 on the site of the Palazzo Reale stables that were destroyed by WWII bombs, PAC was one of Milan's most significant examples of mid-century architecture. It was itself destroyed by a Mafia bomb in 1993 and its rebuilding in 1996 was quixotically faithful to the original. Now it mounts experimental exhibitions in all media. (PAC; 02 7600 9085; www.comune.milano.it/pac; Via Palestro 14; 2.30-7.30pm Mon, 9.30am-7.30pm Tue-Sun; Palestro)

Museo Civico di Storia Naturale

MUSEUM

5 Map p44, D3

Giovanni Ceruti's extravagant Moorish museum was one of the first buildings erected in the public park in 1838. It was built to house the collections of botanist Giorgio Jan and naturalist Giuseppe de Cristoforis, which cover all sorts of things from botany and mineralogy to geology and paleontology. Now its diorama displays are charmingly retro, but younger kids love it. (Natural History Museum; 02 8846 3280; www.comune.milano.it/museostorianaturale; Corso Venezia, 55; adult/reduced €3/1.50; 9am-5.30pm Tue-Sun; ; Palestro)

Spazio Oberdan

GALLERY, CINEMA

6 Map p44, E3

The riches of Milan's *Cineteca* (cinematheque, or film library) are screened downstairs, while upstairs there's a program of exhibitions from stills to video art. The original cinema was redesigned by architect Gae Aulenti, better known for her work on Paris' Musée d'Orsay. (02 7740 6300; www.cinetecamilano.it; Viale Vittorio Veneto 2; exhibitions 2-5pm Tue-Sun, screenings 5-9.30pm Wed-Fri, 3-9.30pm Sat, 11am-9.30pm Sun; Porta Venezia)

E'SPA at Gianfranco Ferré

SPA

7 Map p44, C4

Luxurious surrounds – waxed stucco and shiny wood walls, a Bisazza glass-mosaic floor in black and gold, a private garden – aim for 'refound sensuousness'. Forget about wrinkles and detox, and just enjoy the moment: chromatherapy lights turn your shower into a liquid rainbow, and subtle aromatic oils pervade the air. (☎ 02 7601 7526; www.gianfrancoferre.com; Via Sant'Andrea 15; ⏰ 10am-10pm Tue-Fri, 10am-9pm Sat, 11am-8pm Sun; M San Babila)

Spiga 8 Spa at Hotel Baglioni
SPA

8 ◉　Map p44, D4

Promising to give you back the 'splendour of your youth', Laura Elos' Spiga 8 Spa at the Baglioni has a minimalist all-white aesthetic and a menu of treatments that seem good enough to eat. Try the chocolate facial. (☎ 02 4547 3111; www.baglionihotels.com; Via della Spiga 8; treatments from €70; M San Babila)

Eating

Il Teatro
ITALIAN €€€

9 　Map p44, C4

Service in Il Teatro's opulent formal dining room within the Four Seasons Hotel is disarmingly, unexpectedly warm and the menu sings with surprisingly smart, unfussy offerings and regional flair. Artisanal products and seasonal ingredients feature and there's a daily tasting menu, too. (☎ 02 7 70 88; www.fourseasons.com/milan; Via Gesù 6/8; meals €65-90; ⏰ 7.30-11pm Mon-Sat, 11.45am-3pm Sun mid-Sep–mid-Jul; P ❄ ; M Montenapoleone)

Trattoria Temperanza 'Da Abele'
TRATTORIA €

10 　Map p44, H1

This traditional trattoria with its spartan decor, paper table mats and black-and-white photographs has dedicated itself to the pursuit of the perfect risotto. Here you can try more than 100 different kinds of risotto alongside other traditional dishes such as *brasato* (braised stew). (☎ 02 261 38 55; Via Temperanza 5; risotto €9; ⏰ 8pm-1am Tue-Sun; ✈ ⛻ ; M Pasteur)

Lon Fon
CHINESE €€

11 　Map p44, D2

You can be sure of beautiful veal and onion dumplings, crisp spring rolls and steamed fish with ginger at this buzzing Cantonese restaurant. It's run by mother and daughter team, Rita

---

☑ Top Tip

'House-Museum' card

The **Casemuseocard** (www.case museomilano.it; €15) gives discounted access to Milan's three historical houses: the Bagatti Valsecchi palazzo (p51), the Piero Portaluppi–designed Villa Necchi Campiglio (p35) and the 19th-century Poldi-Pezzoli (p46). Valid for six months, it also entitles the bearer to 10% off in the museum bookshops. You can purchase the card at any of the houses.

and Pui, and they're happy to improvise with seasonal ingredients, such as artichokes. (02 2940 5153; Via Lazzaretto 10; mains €30-45; noon-3pm & 7-11.30pm; M Repubblica)

Joia
ITALIAN, VEGETARIAN €€€

 12 Map p44, D2

Known for seasonal produce and light, clean flavours, the menu at Joia is also imbued with drama and poetry (a winter dish of globe and Jerusalem artichokes, sweet black salsify and pomegranate is entitled 'Beneath a snowy white carpet'). There's the odd overwrought clanger but after one too many servings of leaden *cotoletta* (breaded veal cutlets), chef Pietro Leeman's green realm is nothing short of delightful. (02 2952 2124; www.joia.it; Via Panfilo Castaldi 18; mains €60-80; noon-2.30pm Mon-Fri, 7.30pm-midnight Mon-Sat; M Porta Venezia)

Pizzeria Spontini
PIZZERIA €

13 Map p44, G1

A hot slice isn't a fall back but a first-rate choice at this wood-fired pizza *al trancio* (by the slice) place. The frosted-glass chrome decor may be new, but traditionalists need harbour no concerns: this is the same dough recipe that's responsible for rejuvenating Corso Buenos Aires shoppers since 1953. (02 204 74 44; www .pizzeriaspontini.it; Corso Buenos Aires 60; pizza slice €5; noon-2.30pm & 6-11.30pm; ; M Lima)

Drinking

Pandenus
BAR

 14 Map p44, E2

Originally a bakery, Pandenus was named after the walnut bread that used to emerge from its still active oven. Now the focaccia, pizzetta and bruschetta on its burgeoning *aperitivo* bar, which also features omelettes, couscous and salads, are some of the best in town. Given its proximity to the Marconi Foundation, expect an arty crowd who come for the free wi-fi and weekend brunch. (02 2952 8016; www.pandenus.it; Via A Tadino 15; cocktails/brunch €8/20; 7am-10pm; ; M Porta Venezia)

HClub
BAR, RESTAURANT

 15 Map p44, E3

Secreted behind a vast leather curtain at the back of the Sheraton, the *aperitivo* in the Diana garden is one of Milan's most varied. Grab a freshly crushed peach Bellini and lounge around the low-lit garden. On Tuesday, Wednesday and Thursday it features international music and on Saturday and Sunday it serves brunch. (Diana Garden; 02 2058 2034; www.hclub -diana.com; Viale Piave 42; cocktails/brunch €10/33; 10am-1am; M Porta Venezia)

La Belle Aurore
BAR

 16 Map p44, G4

A local favourite, this old-style bar recalls the city of Buenos Aires with

Understand
Fashion City

Cobblers, seamstresses, tailors and milliners, Italy's artisans have been shoeing, dressing and adorning Europe's affluent classes with the finest fashion money can buy since the 11th century.

The Renaissance
As the Renaissance shone its light on art, music and literature, so fashion flourished, promoted by the celebrities of the day, the Florentine Medicis. Ostentatious fashion dictated status and wealth: hats, snoods, cauls and other headdresses were swagged, draped and jewelled; while gowns had sweeping floor-length sleeves and were made of fine linens, silks, brocades and lace. Styles were borrowed, adapted and disseminated throughout Italy and beyond. In France, the high-heeled shoe was adopted after Catherine de Medici became Queen of France in 1547.

From Florence to Milan
Although the Italian fashion scene originated in Florence, the rigidly controlled salons stifled creativity and forced designers to look elsewhere. Breaking with tradition, Walter Albini held his first show in Milan in 1971. Away from the establishment, he was able to experiment, producing his first ready-to-wear collection and enhancing the role of the designer as the creative force behind the brand. It was a resounding success and from then on Milan began to eclipse Florence as the fashion capital of Italy.

Fashion Capital
Milan's rise to global fashion mecca was far from random. First, thanks to its geographic position, the city had historically strong links with European markets. It was also Italy's capital of finance, advertising, TV and publishing, with both *Vogue* and *Amica* magazines based in the city. What's more Milan had always had a clothing industry based on the historical textile and silk production of upper Lombardy. And, with the city's particular postwar focus on trade fairs, it provided a natural marketplace for the exchange of goods, ideas and information. As a result, by the 1980s a new generation of designers – Armani, Versace, Prada, Ferragamo, Dolce & Gabbana – emerged to conquer the world, transforming shoes, bags, fragrances and sunglasses into the new badges of status and wealth.

bistro tables and ocean liner posters. It attracts a laid-back, diverse crowd from breakfast through to *aperitivo* and late-night wine-soaked chats. There's outdoor seating on the tree-lined pavement in summer. (☏02 2940 6212; Via P G Abamonti 1; ⏰8.30-2am Mon-Sat; Ⓜ Porta Venezia, 🚋9, 23)

Torrefazione Il Caffè Ambrosiano

CAFE, DELICATESSEN

17 Map p44, F2

Inside this *torrefazione* (coffee roaster) there's no seating, just the best coffee in Milan. Stand at the wooden bar and try not to buy something from the retro, sweet-filled cabinets. In summer there is pavement seating on Corso Buenos Aires, where you can sit and watch the world go buy. There's another branch on Corso XXII Marzo 18. (☏02 2952 5069; www.torrefazione ambrosiano.it; Corso Buenos Aires 20; ⏰7am-8pm; Ⓜ Porta Venezia)

L'Elephante

BAR

18 Map p44, F3

The arty-alternative crowd here is as mixed as its killer cocktails: gay, lesbian and straight, locals and visitors. The grungy interior is dominated by shades of night: black, metallic grey and deep purple. (☏02 2951 8768; Via Melzo 22; ⏰6.30pm-2am Tue-Sun; Ⓜ Porta Venezia)

Bar Basso

BAR

19 Map p44, H2

This elegant corner bar is home of the *sbagliato*, the 'incorrect' Negroni made with Prosecco instead of gin, as well as the brilliant concept of *mangia e bevi* (eat and drink), involving a supersized goblet of strawberries, cream and *nocciola* (hazelnut) ice cream and a large slug of some kind of booze. (☏02 2940 0580; www.barbasso.com; Via Plinio 39; ⏰9am-2am Wed-Mon; Ⓜ Lima)

Armani Privé

CLUB

20 Map p44, B4

In the basement of the Armani superstore, this club has a subtle Japanese-Modernist aesthetic, the calm of which you'll need after the hysteria of getting in and clocking the drink prices (€20). Boobs, botox and blonde hair (or a dinner booking at Nobu) will help with the door police. (☏02 6231 2655; Via Gastone Pisoni 1; ⏰10.30pm-2am Tue-Sat Sep-Jun; Ⓜ Montenapoleone)

Shopping

Aspesi

FASHION

21 Map p44, C5

The size of this Antonio Citterio–designed shop is a clue to just how much Italians love this label; Aspesi outerwear is *de rigueur* for mountain and lake weekends and the prices are surprisingly affordable for the Quad. (☏02 7602 2478; www.aspesi.com; Via Monte

LONELY PLANET/GETTY IMAGES©

Necklace display, Pellini

Napoleone 13; ⏲10am-7pm Mon-Sat; Ⓜ San Babila)

Car Shoe
SHOES

22 🅐 Map p44, D5

Founded in 1963 by racecar enthusiast Gianni Mostile, Car Shoe's handmade moccasin with its tiny rubber nubs (so your foot won't slip on the pedal) earned a patent from the Italian Ministry of Industry and Trade as well as a cult following among powerful style icons such as JFK. To counter the lothario rep, it now also does ranges for women and kids. (☎02 7602 4027; www.carshoe.com; Via Della Spiga 1; ⏲10am-7.30pm Mon-Sat, 11am-7pm Sun; Ⓜ San Babila)

Casadei
SHOES

23 🅐 Map p44, C5

Casadei's new signature shoe is called the 'Blade', a dangerous looking steel-heeled beauty in candy colours: lime green, lemon and orange. Milanese girls dream of these hip, but surprisingly wearable, beauties, which are placed on pedestals (literally) in an all-white temple on Via Sant'Andrea. (☎02 7631 8293; www.casadei.com; Via Sant'Andrea 1; ⏲10am-7pm; Ⓜ San Babila)

Driade
FURNITURE, DESIGN

24 🅐 Map p44, C4

Frescoed rooms present the ultimate design challenge – with all those cherubim flying around, suddenly that houndstooth sofa seems a bit too much – but Driade rises to the occasion in its own converted neoclassical palazzo with impeccable eclecticism, unconventional materials and top international designers. (☎02 7602 0359; www.driade.com; Via Manzoni 30; ⏲10am-7pm Tue-Fri, 3-7pm Mon; Ⓜ Montenapoleone)

Etro
FASHION, HOMEWARES

25 🅐 Map p44, C5

Etro's bold paisley prints are a common feature of aristocratic homes. Started as a homewares brand in 1969, they've since branched out into men's and women's fashion. Lay your hands on their signature cashmeres for discount prices at the outlet store on Via Spartaco 3. (☎02 7600 5049; www.etro.it; Via Monte Napoleone 5; ⏲10am-7.30pm; Ⓜ San Babila)

Gallo
FASHION, ACCESSORIES

26 🔒 Map p44, B4

Gallo may spice up its seasonal collections but it's the perennial striped knee-socks that Milanese managers love for adding secret colour to drab business attire. The range for men, women, children and babes is as equally wide and utilises fine silk, cashmere and cotton yarns. (📞02 78 36 02; www.gallospa.it; Via Manzoni 16; ⏱10am-7pm; MMontenapoleone)

Habits Culti
HOMEWARES, FASHION

27 🔒 Map p44, D4

Culti's minimalist homewares retain a tactile earthiness. The range of linen placemats, blond-wood kitchen imple-

✓ Top Tip

Milan Fashion Weeks

Glimpse the future of wardrobes worldwide four times a year, when designers parade next season's collections at the seasonal Milan Fashion Weeks.

The men's shows head the A/W (autumn/winter) schedule in January, with the women's following in February. Men's S/S (spring/summer) take place in June and the women's in September.

For event listings and a full timetable of designer showcases, check with the **Camera Nazionale della Moda Italiana** (National Chamber of Italian Fashion; www.cameramoda.it/eng).

ments, room fragrances and crumpled tunics can prove addictive. (📞02 78 06 37; www.habitsculti.it; Corso Venezia 53; ⏱10am-7pm Mon-Sat; MPalestro) The **spa** (📞02 485 17 588; www.cultidayspa.it; Via Angelo Mauri 5; manicure from €80; ⏱11am-10pm Mon-Sat, 10am-8pm Sun; MConciliazione) is on Via Angelo Mauri.

Pellini
JEWELLERY, ACCESSORIES

28 🔒 Map p44, B4

For one-off pieces of costume jewellery, bags and hair fascinators, look no further than Donatella Pellini's boutique. The Pellini women have been making jewellery for three generations – Donatella's grandmother is famous costume designer Emma Pellini – and their fanciful, handmade creations are not only beautiful but surprisingly affordable, too. (📞02 7600 8084; www.pellini.it; Via Manzoni 20; ⏱3.30-7.30pm Mon, 9.30am-7.30pm Tue-Sat Sep-Jul; MMontenapoleone)

Sermoneta
ACCESSORIES

29 🔒 Map p44, C4

A hole in the wall on chic Via della Spiga, Sermoneta's boutique shop sells standards such as hand-stitched calf-skin gloves alongside more unusual styles made of pony skin or peccary hide. (📞02 7631 8993; www.sermonetagloves.com; Via della Spiga 46; MMontenapoleone)

Explore

Brera

Brera's tight cobbled streets and ancient buildings are a reminder that Milan wasn't always a modern metropolis. At the area's heart is the 17th-century Palazzo di Brera, originally a Jesuit college and now home to the Accademia di Belle Arti, the city's famous art school. Around it are galleries, some of the city's most fashionable restaurants, lively bars and innovative shops. Pretty Via Madonnina is a particular highlight.

The Sights in a Day

Get to **Princi** (p67) before the 10am scrum and order a lavish breakfast of mini *cornetti* filled with hazelnut chocolate and jewel-like fruit tarts to eat alfresco in the piazza. Then take a leisurely stroll south to the **Pinacoteca di Brera** (p60) for a morning browsing Napoleon's superbly curated collection of Old Masters. The artworks are displayed in schools of style, in line with the original intention of the gallery, which was to complement courses at the academy.

The number of treasures in the Pinacoteca can be overwhelming, so take a break and join the dreadlocked students downstairs in the on-site cafe. Alternatively, head down Via Pontaccio for a stand-up meal of cheese and salami at the olive oil bar **Chiù** (p67).

In the early evening stick your head into **Basilica di San Simpliciano** (p65), which often hosts classical music and choral ensembles. Then, if you're dressed to impress, push on to the **Bulgari** (p67) for the most stylish *aperitivo* in town, overlooking the manicured private garden.

Top Sights

Pinacoteca di Brera (p60)

Best of Milan

Art
Pinacoteca di Brera (p60)

Eating
Maxelâ (p66)

Pescheria da Claudio (p67)

Ristorante Solferino (p66)

Latteria di San Marco (p66)

Fashion
La Vetrina di Beryl (p70)

Drinking
Bulgari Hotel (p67)

N'Ombra de Vin (p68)

Bookshop & Caffeteria degli Atellani (p68)

Getting There

M Metro Brera is bounded by four metro stops. The best for the Pinacoteca is Montenapoleone on MM3 (yellow line) and Lanza on MM2 (green line). For the shops and restaurants to the north, use Moscova on line MM2 (green).

Tram No 1 gives good access to the shopping street Via Vetero.

Top Sights
Pinacoteca di Brera

Located upstairs from the Brera Academy (still one of Italy's most prestigious art schools), this gallery houses Milan's impressive collection of Old Masters, much of it 'lifted' from Venice by Napoleon. Rembrandt, Goya and van Dyck all have a place in the collection, but you're here to see the Italians: Titian, Tintoretto, Veronese and the Bellini brothers. Much of the work has tremendous emotional clout, most notably Mantegna's brutal *Cristo morto nel Sepolcro e tre Dolenti* (Lamentation over the Dead Christ).

◉ Map p64, C4

☏ 02 7226 3264

www.brera.beniculturali.it

Via Brera 28

adult/reduced €6/3

🕑 8.30am-7.15pm Tue-Sun

Ⓜ Lanza

Interior, Pinacoteca di Brera

Don't Miss

Lombard Frescoes
The Brera collection starts with a blast of Renaissance brilliance, launching you down a corridor lined with Donato Bramante's *Men at Arms* and Bernardino Luini's frescoes from the suppressed church of La Pace and Casa Pelucca. While Luini's tableau of girls playing 'hot-cockles' and the Easter feast illustrate the influence of Leonardo da Vinci – blending Renaissance innovations with indigenous Milanese scenes – Bramante's soldiers, meant for the Barons' Hall at Casa Visconti, define a new understanding of illusionistic perspective. Viewed from below (as they would have been in the hall), the figures loom upwards, their gigantic forms emerging from architectural frames.

Oratorio di Mocchirolo
To the left side of the entrance hall in Room IA is a reconstruction of the oratory of Mocchirolo and its splendid fresco cycle, thought to be the work of Giotto. Particularly notable is the *Crucifixion* scene, which displays Giotto's typically strong sense of visual narrative and expressive realism.

Bellini & Mantegna
The works of Giovanni Bellini and Andrea Mantegna, displayed in room VI, are some of the highlights of the Pinacoteca's Venetians. Like Bramante before him, Mantegna had a passion for rigorous perspective and a love of classicism that combined to create the stunningly unsentimental *Lamentation over the Dead Christ*, with its violent foreshortening of Christ's corpse. Although influenced by Mantegna, Bellini's sad-eyed Madonnas and exquisitely tender *Pietà* demonstrate the progressing humanisation of

☑ Top Tips

▶ You'll need at least half a day to cover the gallery's 38 rooms at a reasonable pace.

▶ The gallery is upstairs on the 1st floor. Stairs are behind Canova's bronze statue of Napoleon posing as a demigod in the courtyard.

▶ Audio guides are available in Italian, French, English, Spanish and German for €5.

▶ Don't miss the glass-walled restoration laboratory, where you can see conservators at work.

✗ Take a Break

The Pinacoteca's treasures can be overwhelming, so head downstairs and join life-drawing students for a post-class Peroni.

For a light lunch, stand at the olive bar at Chiù (p67) to sample plates of cheese and salami with regional oils; or in the evening wander up to N'Ombra de Vin (p68) for wine tastings and bistro fare.

the subject, enhanced by the expressive effects of colour and light in the landscape around them.

Titian, Veronese & Tintoretto

The high-water mark of the Renaissance dawned in Venice in the 16th century with an extraordinary confluence of talent in the persons of Tizian Vercelli (Titian), Paolo Veronese and Jacopo Tintoretto. While Rome was in decline and the rest of Italy oppressed by moral mores that the licentious Venetians scoffed at, Venice had both the deep pockets of the Doge and his stabilising iron rule. So wealth, patronage and art flourished, with Titian as protagonist. Room IX brings together some of the period's greatest works, including Titian's *St Jerome*

and Veronese's *Cena in Casa di Simone* (Supper in the House of Simon).

The Jesi Collection: 20th Century

Off room VIII is the Jesi Collection, donated in 1984. It includes the 12 sculptures and 68 paintings of Emilio Jesi, acquired in the 1930s, '40s and '50s. A welcome relief from the main gallery's religious pieces, these vibrant Futurist canvases include Boccioni's fabulous *Rissa in Galleria* (Riot in the Gallery) and Carlo Carrà's *La Musa Metafisica* (Metaphysical Muse).

The Urbino School

One of the greatest painters of the early Renaissance, Piero della Francesca was engaged by Urbino's Count

PINOTECA DI BRERA

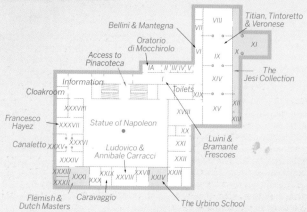

of Montefeltro in 1474. Although the Tuscan artist and mathematician is more famous for his cycle of frescoes depicting the *Legend of the True Cross* in Arezzo's Basilica di San Francesco, the monumental Montefeltro altarpiece, otherwise known as the *Brera Madonna* (1472–74), is the prize of room XXIV. As a counterpoint, take a look at Raphael's much looser and more natural *Wedding of the Virgin,* which was painted in 1504.

Caravaggio
From the darkening palate and glimmering colours of the Baroque Emilian school of the late 16th and early 17th centuries, you're barely prepared for the emotional thump that room XXIX delivers. Home to the academy's only Caravaggio, *Cena in Emmaus* (Supper at Emmaus), the room is dark and brooding. Gone is the neat formal classicism of Raphael and the Mannerist trickery of Carracci, and in its place is a potent, weighty naturalism, framed by an existential conflict between light and dark.

Flemish Masters
Amid its huge Italian collection, the academy inherited a small selection of Flemish and Dutch masters, now housed in rooms XXXI through XXXIII. Rubens, Rembrandt and Van Dyck arrived from the Louvre in 1813 and in 1855 Peter Oggioni donated masters of the Antwerp school, Jan de Beer, along with German artists Herman Rode and Hans Memling. Seen in the context of all that has gone before,

FOTOTECA STORICA NAZIONALE ©

The Kiss by Francesco Hayez (1859)

the cross-pollination from the Renaissance is particularly noticeable.

The 19th Century
By the time you reach the final rooms and the early 19th century, when the gallery itself was gaining prominence, the artwork becomes lighter, imbued with the Romanticism and patriotism of post-unified Italy. Breeze through Canaletto's atmospheric views of Venice to Francesco Hayez, pet portrait artist for the Lombard nobility and a director at the Academy. They include the intense and luminous *Il Bacio* (The Kiss; 1859), one of the most reproduced artworks in the gallery, which came to symbolise the hopes of the Risorgimento.

A   B   C   D

Bastioni di Porta Nuova

1

Bastioni di Porta Volta

Via Marsala

Via Solferino

4 ✕

For reviews see
- ⊙ Top Sights
- ⊙ Sights
- ✕ Eating
- ⊙ Drinking
- ✪ Entertainment
- 🔒 Shopping

Largo La Foppa 🔒15

✕10

Moscova Ⓜ ✕7

6 ✕

Via San Marco

Mediateca di Santa Teresa

🔒11

13 🔒

Via della Moscova

2

Via Legnano

Corso Garibaldi

Via Statuto

🔒19

Via Solferino

5 ✕

Via Palermo

Via Montebello

18 🔒

Via San Marco

Via Cernaia

3

Basilica di San Simpliciano

⊙2

🔒12

Via Fatebenefratelli

Via dell'Anunciata

Via Principe Amede

Piccolo Teatro Strehler

✪14

Ⓜ Lanza

BRERA

Via Pontaccio 9 ✕

Via Fiori Chiari

Via Fiori Oscuri

4

Via Mercato

Via Madonnina

⊙ **Pinacoteca di Brera**

Via dei Giardini

Via Gast Pisto

Foro Buonaparte

Via Arco

Via Ponte Vetero

⊙1
Orto Botanico

Via Brera

⊙3
Bulgari Spa

Piazza Croce Rossa

Ⓜ Montenapo

Castle Sforzesco

17🔒

20🔒
16🔒

Via Monte di Pietà

QUADRILATERO D'ORO

5

21🔒

8✕

Via Broletto

Via dell'Orso

Via Cusani

Ⓜ Cairoli

Ⓝ 0 ———— 200 r
     0 ———— 0.1 miles

Sights

Orto Botanico
GARDENS

1 ⊙ Map p64, C4

Maria Teresa had the towering gingko tree planted here in 1777, when she turned the former Jesuit veggie patch into an open-air lecture hall for budding botanists (the wunderkind of the Enlightenment). This fragrant, walled garden is still filled with medicinal plants and is a perfect nature fix after the cultural onslaught of the Pinacoteca. (Via Brera 28; admission free; ⊙9am-noon & 1-4pm Mon-Fri; Ⓜ Montenapoleone)

Basilica di San Simpliciano
CHURCH

2 ⊙ Map p64, B3

San Simpliciano is one of St Ambrose's four Milanese churches, built on a paleo-Christian cemetery with a red-brick Romanesque wrapping. Martyrs Sisinio, Martirio and Alessandro are buried here, and supposedly rose from their graves in the form of doves to give courage to the Lombard League in the battle of Legnano (1176), leading to the defeat of Barbarossa. The beautiful fresco in the apse is Bergognone's *Coronation of the Virgin* (1515). (☎02 86 22 74; www.sansimpliciano.it; Piazza San Simpliciano 7;

Basilica di San Simpliciano

admission free; ⏱ 9am-noon & 2.15-7pm Mon-Fri, 9.30am-7pm Sat & Sun; Ⓜ Lanza)

Bulgari Spa   SPA

3 ◉ Map p64, C5

This warm, enveloping space in the basement of the Antonio Cittero–designed hotel instils immediate calm. Espa aromatherapy treatments target pressure points and chakras. Make sure to amortise the sky-high prices with a dip in the gorgeous gold-mosaic-lined pool or a lounge in the ethereal steam room. (📞 02 805 80 51; www.bulgarihotel.com; Via Privata Fratelli Gabba 7b; Ⓜ Montenapoleone)

Eating

Shiki   JAPANESE €€

4 🍽 Map p64, C1

Elegant Shiki, with its white-on-black decor, silky drapes and glinting chandeliers, feels like a decadent Parisian salon. The well-structured menu and wine list has the Milanese literally cooing over it: 'Such fresh clams; the quality of the *crudo!*' No wonder city diginatries and fashionistas choose to eat here. (📞 02 2900 3345; www.shikimilano.it; Via Solferino 35; meals €35-45; ⏱ noon-3pm Mon-Fri, 8pm-2am daily; ❄; Ⓜ Moscova)

Latteria di San Marco   TRATTORIA €

5 🍽 Map p64, C2

If you can snare a seat in this tiny and ever-popular restaurant (originally a dairy shop), you'll find old favourites such as *spaghetti alla carbonara* mixed in with chef Arturo's own creations, including *polpettine al limone* (little meatballs with lemon) or *riso al salto* (risotto fritters) on the ever-changing, mostly organic menu. (📞 02 659 76 53; Via San Marco 24; meals €18-25; ⏱ 7-11pm Mon-Fri; ♿; Ⓜ Moscova)

Ristorante Solferino   MILANESE €€€

6 🍽 Map p64, C1

Salivary glands have worked overtime here for a century, thanks to hearty classics such as osso bucco swathed in risotto, unexpected delights in fish tortelloni, and an extensive vegetarian menu. Join Italian film stars risking their girlish figures with the in-house pastry chef's creations, and journalists steadily losing their objectivity over a superior wine selection. (📞 02 2900 5748; www.ilsolferino.com; Via Castelfidardo 2; meals €45-60; ❄ 🍷; Ⓜ Moscova)

Maxelâ   STEAKHOUSE €€

7 🍽 Map p64, B2

Come with a hearty appetite and order Maxelâ's 1kg *bistecca Fiorentina*. When it arrives, don't baulk at the size: the first bite of that velvety soft Fassone beef sprinkled with salt crystals will make you want to weep with joy. Come with friends and order more: try the delicately flavoured *carpaccio* (finely sliced raw beef) and the artisanal salami. (📞 02 2906 2926; www.maxela.it; Via della Moscova 50; meals €18-30; ❄; Ⓜ Moscova)

Local Life
Raw Like Sushi

Italians love their *crudo* (raw seafood) almost as much as the Japanese. *Crudo*'s appeal draws on the same taste and texture elements as sushi – a deceptively simple balance of fat, salt and acid – but uses olive oil, vinegar or citrus, sea salt and pepper instead of soy, pickle and wasabi. The Milanese can't get enough, whether it's Italian-style, trad Japanese or a fusion of the two, and strangely often refer to all forms of *crudo* as 'sushi'. For fabulously fresh and simple fish, try Da Claudio (p67), do smart sushi and sashimi at Sushi Koboo (p110), and for a deluxe Milanese-Japanese fusion twist head to Zero (p99) or Shiki (p66).

Pescheria da Claudio   SEAFOOD €€

8   Map p64, B5

Join the savvy suits for a power lunch or early dinner of *pesce crudo* (raw fish). Plates loaded with marinated tuna, mixed salmon, tuna and white fish with pistachios or lightly blanched octopus *carpaccio* are consumed standing along bars facing the fishmonger's produce, with a glass of light fizz. For a more leisurely lunch, dine upstairs in the sleek white-on-black restaurant. (☑02 805 68 57; www .pescheriadaclaudio.it; Via Cusani 1; meals €35-55; ⏰8.30am-2.30pm & 4-9pm Tue-Sat; ❄; Ⓜ Cairoli, 🚊3, 4)

Chiù   MOZZARELLA BAR, DELI €

9   Map p64, B4

Specialist delicatessen Chiù serves up Milan's best *mozzarella di bufala* and *burrata* cheeses, sourced straight from producers in Campania. Order a plate with prociutto and *caponata* (aubergine salad) and stand at the olive oil bar dunking bread in liquid gold and savouring the cool, creamy texture. (☑02 805 22 96; Via Pontaccio 5; meals €8-15; ⏰10.30am-3pm & 4.30-8pm Tue-Fri, to 6.30pm Mon & Sat; ❄; Ⓜ Lanza)

Princi   BAKERY €

10   Map p64, B1

Not all Princi branches are created equal. This one is blessed with the same beautiful Claudio Silvestrin design as its Via Speronari sister, and is open similarly long hours, giving you lots of opportunities to sample their artisanal range of pastries, Stracchino-filled focaccia and fruit-filled tarts. (☑02 2906 0832; www.princi.it; Piazza XXV Aprile 5; pastries from €2.50; ⏰7am-2am; Ⓜ Moscova, Garibaldi)

Drinking

Bulgari Hotel   HOTEL BAR

3   Map p64, C5

Whether it's inside beneath the giant botanical sculptures at the earth-toned bar or outside on the terrace overlooking the brilliantly green garden, the *aperitivo* scene here is

Piccolo Teatro Strehler

an intense slice of Milan life. The second-cheapest wine on the list may weigh in at €20, but it's cheap for the theatre, darling. (📞02 805 80 51; www.bulgarihotel.com; Via Privata Fratelli Gabba 7/b; 🕙7.30am-1am; Ⓜ Montenapoleone)

Bookshop & Caffeteria degli Atellani
CAFE, BAR

11 Map p64, C2

Next to the Santa Teresa Mediateca digital library, Cafe Atellani is one of Milan's best bars. Known simply as Il Cubo (the Cube), its glasshouse design is modelled on a tropical greenhouse and overlooks a tranquil garden. Inside the long sleek bar is lined with

an extensive selection of Italian wines, which you can enjoy with light, contemporary plates after a browse in the cinema bookshop. (📞02 3653 5959; www.atellani.it; Via della Moscova 28; 🕙8.30am-9.30pm Mon-Fri, 9.30am-7.30pm Sat & Sun; 🛜; Ⓜ Moscova)

N'Ombra de Vin
ENOTECA

12 Map p64, C3

This wine bar is located in a former Augustine refectory, and it retains a Catholic approach to the fruit of the vine. Tastings can be had at any time of the day and there's also a small bistro if all that swilling sees you work up a decent appetite. The classic risotto Milanese is topped with artichoke and breadcrumbs, while white asparagus spears are served with quail eggs. (📞02 659 96 50; www .nombradevin.it; Via San Marco 2; ⊗9am-midnight Mon-Sat; Ⓜ️Moscova)

Moscatelli BAR

 13 Map p64, A2

It may have been open since the 19th-century Franco-Austrian war, but the decor at this popular bar belongs firmly in the 1950s. It's all about the wine here, and maybe a plate of *coppa* (cured pork neck) and some bread. (📞02 655 46 02; Corso Garibaldi 93; ⊗8am-1am Mon-Sat; Ⓜ️Moscova)

Entertainment

Piccolo Teatro Strehler THEATRE

14 ⭐ Map p64, A4

This Marco Zanuso–designed theatre was opened amid much fanfare more than 10 years ago to address the capacity restraints of the original incarnation; and it has gone on to establish itself as one of Milan's cultural powerhouses. The sprawling complex includes the Teatro Studio at Via Rivoli 6. (📞02 4241 1889; www .piccoloteatro.org; Largo Greppi; ⊗box office 10am-6.45pm Mon-Sat, 1-6.30pm Sun; Ⓜ️Lanza)

Shopping

asap FASHION

15 🔒 Map p64, B1

Locally sourced, recycled jersey, cashmere and leather are the base materials of asap (as sustainable as possible). The pieces are not just gorgeously detailed, cool and unique, but they also question fashion's endlessly recurring cycle of excitement and oblivion. What else would a smart girl wear? (📞02 659 81 57; www .asaplab.it; Corso Garibaldi 104; ⊗3.30-7.30pm Mon, 10.30am-7.30pm Tue-Fri; Ⓜ️Moscova)

Cavalli e Nastri CLOTHING

16 🔒 Map p64, C5

The Milanese took a while to take to vintage ('Won't people think I'm poor?' 'How will anyone know what label it is?'), but this colourful shop

 Local Life
Fashionable Art
Beyond Brera's independent galleries, a number of dynamic private *fondazione* (foundations) champion some of the city's most avant-garde art. Fondazione Prada (p108), **Trussardi** (📞02 806 88 21; www.fondazion enicolatrussardi.com; Piazza della Scala 5) and Fondazione Arnaldo Pomodoro (p115) all stage programs of important, ground-breaking work. These shows are well worth looking out for; they're attention grabbing in scale and often competitive in the provocation stakes.

in the heart of Brera has led the way. Stock is mostly sourced from legendary early and mid 20th-century Italian fashion houses. (☏02 7200 0449; www.cavallienastri.com; Via Brera 2; ⏰10am-7pm; ⓂPonte Vetero)

Fabriano
STATIONERY, ACCESSORIES

17 🔒 Map p64, B5

Stationery-tragics won't be the only ones going quietly ga-ga over Fabriano's goods. Everything from plain notebooks to linen pencil cases and kooky leather keyrings are exquisitely crafted. Staff are delightful and wrap gifts with trademark flair. (☏02 7631 8754; www.fabrianoboutique.com; Via Ponte

Vetero 17; ⏰1-7.30pm Mon, 10am-7.30pm Tue-Sat; ⓂCairoli, 🚇1)

Kristina Ti
FASHION

18 🔒 Map p64, B3

Kristina Ti specialises in pieces that are swooningly pretty but never one-dimensionally girly. Slips and lingerie can be nicely boxed as gifts. (☏02 65 33 79; www.kristinati.com; Via Solferino 18; ⏰10am-7pm; ⓂMoscova)

La Vetrina di Beryl
SHOES

19 🔒 Map p64, B2

Barbara Beryl's name was known to cultists around the world, way before Manolo became a byword for female

CRISTINA FUMI / ALAMY ©

Carnival by Cherdsak Wangprachanont, 2011 Elephant Parade

desire. Stumbling upon this deceptively nondescript shop is like chancing upon the shoe racks at a *Vogue Italia* photo shoot. There's a rack or two of clothes, too. (☎02 65 42 78; Via Statuto 4; ☺10am-7pm Mon-Sat; Ⓜ Moscova)

Rigadritto
GIFTS

20 🔒 Map p64, C5

Loads of little stickers, clips, pencils and decorated stationery fill this graphic, colourful space. Cat and dog T-shirts that turn humans into pets are delightful. (☎02 8058 2936; www .rigadritto.com; Via Brera 6; ☺10.30am-7.30pm; Ⓜ Montenapoleone)

Zeis House
SHOES

21 🔒 Map p64, A5

Milan's miles of cobblestones and days of drizzle can make the most dedicated heel-wearer weep. Take a cue from locals who don Bikkemberg trainers for day. Patent and metallic options are available for those who refuse to entirely discard glam. (☎02 8691 5563; www.zeisexcelsa.it; Via Cusani 10; ☺10am-7pm Tue-Sun; Ⓜ Cairoli)

Explore

Parco Sempione & Porta Garibaldi

Walk beneath the imposing battlements of Castello Sforzesco en route to one of its museums or the leafy oasis of Parco Sempione, and modern Milan slips away. On the southwestern edge of the park is the imposing Triennale di Milano, and to the northeast the emerging skyscrapers of the Porta Nuova and buzzing Corso Como and Corso Garibaldi, which have a cruisey, southern-Californian feel in summer.

The Sights in a Day

☀ Start the day with the block-buster collection of museums in the Sforza's turreted **Castello** (p76). It houses seven specialised museums, but the standout collection of the Museo d'Arte Antica is not to be missed. Some of its halls were designed by Leonardo da Vinci, and their frescoed decorations compete with intriguing fragments of Milanese history for your attention.

☀ Then pause for lunch in the castle's back garden, now the **Parco Sempione** (p80). Take a seat on the patio or upstairs terrace at **Bar Bianco** (p81). Refuelled, wend your way through the park to the **Triennale di Milano** (p78) or head to architect-designer Achille Castiglioni's **studio** (p82). Afterwards, if the weather's good, climb to the top of Giò Ponti's **Torre Branca** (p81) for views over the leafy loveliness of the park and its ponds.

☾ To kick off the evening either head back to the Design Museum for evening *aperitivo,* or push on to pedestrianised Corso Como for world-class people-watching and stylish cocktails at **10 Corso Como** (p82).

For a local's day in Parco Sempione, see p80.

Top Sights

Castello Sforzesco (p76)

Triennale di Milano (p78)

◌ Local Life

Life in Parco Sempione

♥ Best of Milan

Design

Triennale di Milano (p78)

Studio Museo Achille Castiglioni (p82)

Architecture

Stazione Centrale (p82)

History

Castello Sforzesco (p76)

Cimitero Monumentale (p82)

Gardens

Parco Sempione (p80)

Nightlife

Blue Note (p87)

Getting There

Ⓜ **Metro** MM1 (red line) stops at Cadorna and Cairoli for the Castello and Triennale. For the cemetery, Corso Como and Isola, use Porta Garibaldi on MM2 (green line).

A B C D

20

Via Amm
Francesco
Caracciolo

Via Principe
Eugenio

Via Giuseppe
Govone

Via Valte

1

Via Censio

Via Valte

6

Via Ezio Biondi

Cimitero
Monument

Via Fauché

13

1

Via Losanna

Via Fratelli Induno

Piazzale
Cimitero
Monumentale

18

Via Piero della Francesca

Piazza
Gerusalemme

10

Via Monviso

**PARCO
SEMIONE**

Via Donato Bramante

Via Cere

Via Giulio Cesare Procaccini

Via Messina

2

Corso Sempione

Via Nussi
Via Saronno

9

12

8

14

Chinatow

Via Paolo Sarpi

Via Antonio Rosmini

Viale Montello

Largo Domodossola

Via Luigi Canonica

Via Francesco
Ferruccio

3

Fiera
Milano

Via Andrea Massena

Via Melzi d'Eril

27

Bastioni

Viale Elvezia

11

Arca della Pace

Arena
Civica

Via Canova

Piazza
Sempione

Via Vicenzo Monti

Parco Sempione

Foro
Buonap

4

Via Gabriele Rossetti

17

Piazza Ca

**Triennale
di Milano**

Parco
Pallavicino

Via Ludovico Ariosto

Via Mario Pagano

Viale al Parco
Luigi Camoens

Viale Emilio Alemagna

**Castello
Sforzesco**

Viale Gadio

Studio Museo
Achille Castiglio

Via XX Settembre

2

Piazz
Castell

5

Pagano

Conciliazione

Stazione Nord (Stazione
Cadorna)

Via Giovanni Boccaccio

Cadorna Triennale

E   Piazza 7 16 Piazzale Lagosta   F   G   H   Sondrio

Fidia 15
Via A. della Pergola   21   ISOLA   Via Luigi Galvani

Via Pollaiuolo   Via Sammartini

Via Jacopo del Verme   Via Sebenico   Stazione
                                                                  Centrale
Via Pastrengo 26   Via F. Confalonieri   3

azzoli   Via Gaetano De Castillia   22

5   Stazione   CORSO   Torre Pirelli 4   Piazza Duca
         Porta   GARIBALDI   d'Aosta
         Garibaldi   Gioia Via Giovanni Battista Pirelli   Centrale FS

         Garibaldi   Via Fabio   Via Vittor Pisani   V Napo Torriani
    19   Piazza   Filzi
         Sigmund Freud   Viale della Liberazione
         Via Alessio
   Corso de Tocqueville
le Pasubio Como 5   Via Felice Casati
                                                               Viale Tunisia
ale F Crispi Piazzale XXV Aprile   Via G Galilei
                                                                      Via Panfilo Castaldi
         23   Bastioni di Porta Nuova   Republica
                                              Viale Vittorio Veneto
      Via Marsala Via Castelfidardo   Porta
                                                          Bastioni di Porta Venezia Venezia
Largo   Via C.Mangilli
La Foppa   Porta
cova   Via della Moscova   Venezia

Via Statuto Via Solferino Via San Marco Corso di Porta Nuova
                              Turati

Via Palermo   Via Montebello
                                                     Via D.Manin
Corso Garibaldi

za   Via Pontaccio   BRERA   Via Fatebenefratelli Piazza   Via Palestro
                                                     Cavour
Via Fiori Chiari
                    Via dei Giardini   Turati   Giardini
                                                 Pubblici
                                                               Palestro
24   For reviews see
a Cusani   Top Sights   p76
roli   Via dell'Orso   Sights   p82
                          Eating   p82
        Montenapoleone   Drinking   p85
                          Entertainment   p87   Via Mozart
                          Shopping   p89   SAN
                                                               BABILA
        N 0   500 m
           0   0.25 miles

Via Alessandro
Manzoni

Via Luigi Majno

Top Sights
Castello Sforzesco

Originally a Visconti fortress, this iconic red-brick castle was later home to the mighty Sforza dynasty who ruled Renaissance Milan. The castle's defences were designed by the multitalented da Vinci; Napoleon later drained the moat and removed the drawbridges. Today it shelters seven specialised museums, which gather together intriguing fragments of Milan's cultural and civic history, from the medieval equestrian tomb of Bernabò Visconti to Michelangelo's *Rondanini Pietà*, his final unfinished masterpiece.

Map p74, D5

02 8846 3700

www.milanocastello.it

Piazza Castello

adult/reduced €3/1.50

9am-5.30pm Tue-Sun

Cairoli

Castello Sforzesco

Don't Miss

The Architecture

To withstand any presumptuous challenges to their power, Milan's politicking Sforzas gave the castle its robust medieval layout and character. Francesco invited Florentine architect Filarete to design the high central tower in 1452 to soften the appearance and affect an elegant residence rather than a barracks. Thick round towers, faced with diamond-shaped *serizzo*, bolstered the ramparts, and Galeazzo Maria later embellished the Rochetta and Ducal Courtyard with Renaissance porticos. Inside the ducal apartments were endowed with elegant pavilion vaults, and later decorated by Leonardo da Vinci, under the patronage of Ludovico Sforza (1452–1508).

Civiche Raccolta d'Arte Antica

Housed in the ducal apartments, the Museum of Ancient Art is a stellar collection. From paleo-Christian frescoes to the fine equestrian tomb of Bernarbò Visconti and sculpted reliefs depicting Milan's triumph over Barbarossa, the artworks tell the turbulent story of the birth of Italy's first city *comune,* murderous dynastic and regional ambitions, and lavish artistic patronage. Da Vinci had a hand in the interior decor, which sports coats of arms, murals and the Gonfalcon of the King of Spain who married here in 1555.

Pinacoteca e Raccolte d'Arte

On the 1st floor the Furniture Museum and castle Art Gallery blend seamlessly, leading you from ducal wardrobes and writing desks through to a blockbuster collection of Lombard Gothic art. Among the masterpieces are Andrea Mantegna's *Trivulzio Madonna,* Vincenzo Foppa's *St Sebastian* and Bramantino's *Noli me tangere* (Touch me not).

☑ **Top Tips**

▸ Admission to the castle museums is free Friday (2pm to 5.30pm).

▸ Take a guided tour around the castle walls for a great overview of the complex, the park and even the distant Duomo.

▸ If you're short on time, the best collection is the Civiche Raccolte d'Arte Antica (Museum of Ancient Art), which takes you through the frescoed ducal apartments.

✗ **Take a Break**

If the weather's nice have a picnic in the park or a drink on the terrace of Bar Bianco (p81).

For something more substantial, consider a plate of *crudo* at Pescheria da Claudio (p67); or, in the evening, stroll across the park for *aperitivo* at Living (p85).

Top Sights
Triennale di Milano

Italy's first Triennale took place in 1923 in Monza. It aimed to promote interest in Italian design and the applied arts, from 'the spoon to the city', and its success led to the creation of Giovanni Muzio's Palazzo d'Arte in Milan in 1933. Since then the Triennale has championed design in all its forms, although the triennale formula has since been replaced by long annual events, with international exhibits as part of the program.

Map p74, C4

www.triennaledesign museum.it

Viale Emilio Alemanga 6

adult/reduced €8/6.50

10.30am-8.30pm Tue-Wed & Sat-Sun, to 11pm Thu-Fri

M Cadorna

Interior, Triennale di Milano

Don't Miss

Design Museum

Regular shows in the Triennale building have championed design practice since the 1930s, but its permanent museum of Italian design was only launched in 2007. Across a symbolic bridge, the inaugural survey of iconic objects and furniture included Pesce's Moloch lamp and Sottsass' Memphis pieces. Recent exhibits included Fabio Novembre's 2012 exploration of the Italian school of graphics through a rainbow metaphor where iconic adverts, posters and magazines were displayed in three-dimensional, coloured spaces that acted as a clever visual hypertext for the works on display.

Triennale Bookshop

Located in the sunken impluvium, opposite the grand staircase, the Triennale's **bookshop** (☎02 8901 3403; Viale Emilio Alemagna 6; ⊗10.30am-8.30pm Tue, Wed, Sat & Sun, to 11pm Thu & Fri; ⓂCadorna) is a feast of beautifully produced art, architecture and design editions as enthralling as the exhibitions themselves. Laid out according to Michele De Lucchi's design on large display tables, the room is a social hub, and originally led into an internal courtyard that has since been lost.

Triennale Design Café

Overlooking the Parco Sempione treetops, the Design Café (see right) is a bright white space arranged around a central serving station. In between tables and chairs, donated by local furniture houses, are glass-topped counters displaying temporary exhibits of jewellery and design objects. At one end the industrial kitchen is open to view, screened behind a glass wall. From it ushers (you guessed it) designer food. Opt for the less complex dishes and enjoy the view, both inside and out.

☑ Top Tips

▶ The Triennale is a major venue for the Salone del Mobile in April, and closes for several days during that period to set up the exhibits.

▶ In the garden, seek out de Chirico's *Fontana dei Bagni Misteriosi* (Fountain of Mysterious Baths; 1973).

▶ Check ahead during summer as the museum closes for a month to rotate the exhibits in the Design Museum.

✕ Take a Break

Stop for coffee or lunch in the Triennale's **Design Café** (☎02 87 54 41; www .triennale.it; Viale Alemanga 6; ⊗10.30am-8.30pm Tue-Sun, to 10.30pm Thu; ⓂCadorna), which overlooks the leafy greenery of Parco Sempione.

If you'd rather step outside the Palazzo d'Arte, join the *aperitivo* circus in the Just Cavalli Cafe (p81) beneath the Torre Branca.

Local Life
Life in Parco Sempione

Situated behind the castle, Parco Sempione was once the preserve of hunting Sforza dukes. Then Napoleon came to town and set about landscaping. First the French carved out orchards and then the idea for a public park was mooted in 1891. It was a resounding success, and even today Milanese of all ages come to enjoy its winding paths, shady copses and ornamental ponds.

❶ Arco della Pace

Napoleon's 25m-high triumphal 'Arch of Peace', designed by Luigi Cagnola in 1807, was built on the site of the Roman Porta Giovia (Gate of Jupiter). It marks the start of Corso Sempione that connects Milan to Paris, via the Simplon (Sempione) Pass. Ironically, its neoclassical facade is graced with bas-reliefs not of Napoleon's victories, as was intended, but with scenes from the Battle of Leipzig (1813), depicting

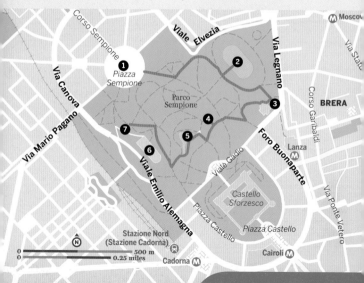

Napoleon's defeat, and the Congress of Vienna (1815), which redrew the post-Napoleonic map of Europe.

❷ Arena Civica

The Arena Civica was Napoleon's mini-colosseum, which he opened in typically flamboyant style with a chariot race in 1807. Built by Luigi Canonica, its ingenious engineering allowed it to be flooded with water from nearby canals to stage mock sea battles. Now it hosts football and rugby matches, along with the annual Notturna di Milano, a track and field event held in September.

❸ Acquario Civico

You'll be transfixed by the aquatic Art-Nouveau facade, but kids will race ahead to see Lombardy's fish on display at Europe's third-oldest **aquarium** (📞02 8846 5750; www.acquariocivicomilano .eu; Viale Gadio 2; admission free; ⏲9am-1pm & 2-5.30pm Tue-Sun; Ⓜ️Lanza). It turns out mountain streams make for rather predictable silver fish, but that only makes the red anemones more flashy.

❹ Bar Bianco

Ricardo Griffini's **Bar Bianco** (📞02 8699 2026; www.bar-bianco.com; Parco Sempione; ⏲7pm-1am Wed & Thu, to 2am Fri & Sat; Ⓜ️Lanza), situated right in the heart of the park, was built for the Tenth Triennale (1954). Still popular for *aperitivo*, it is the most down-to-earth of the Parco bars. The patio seats are good for people-watching, but aim for the upper terrace; it's like having a cocktail in a treehouse.

❺ Ponte delle Sirenette

The 'Bridge of Mermaids' is the park's official lovers' lane. It originally spanned the Naviglio della Martesana (Martesan Canal), which once linked Milan to the river Adda. Filled in during the 1930s, the canal became Via Melchiorre Gioia and the pretty bridge with its cast-iron mermaids was transferred to the park's pond, and now provides the perfect backdrop for dates and proposals.

❻ Palazzo d'Arte

West of the pond looms the enormous Rationalist Palace of Art (aka Triennale di Milano), designed by Giovanni Muzio in 1932–33 to host the burgeoning Triennale exhibitions. Poke your head through the garden grills for a look at de Chirico's bizarre sculpture *Fontana dei Bagni Misteriosi* (Fountain of Mysterious Baths; 1973).

❼ Torre Branca

Giò Ponti's spindly 1933 steel **tower** (📞02 331 41 20; lift €4; Ⓜ️Cadorna), built in just two months for a Triennale exhibition, provides a fantastic 108m-high viewing platform over the park. Operating hours are complex: it's open for blocks of a few hours at a time, generally between 9.30am or 10.30am and midnight; check the the website for details. Take the lift up at sunset, or at night to watch city lights twinkle, and lord it over the crowd below in **Just Cavalli Café** (📞02 31 18 17; www.just cavallicafe.com; Parco Sempione; ⏲8pm-2am Mon-Sun; Ⓜ️Cadorna).

Sights

Cimitero Monumentale CEMETERY

1 ⊙ Map p74, D1

Since 1866, Milan's wealthy have kept their dynastic ambitions alive long after death with grand sculptural gestures behind striking Renaissance-revival black-and-white walls. Nineteenth-century 'death and the maiden' eroticism gives way to some fabulous abstract forms from midcentury masters. Studio BBPR's geometric steel-and-marble memorial to Milan's WWII concentration camp dead is stark and moving. Grab a map inside the forecourt. (☏02 8846 5600; www.monumentale.net; Piazzale Cimitero Monumentale; ⊙8am-6pm Tue-Sun; ⓜGaribaldi)

Studio Museo Achille Castiglioni MUSEUM

2 ⊙ Map p74, D5

Architect, designer and teacher Achille Castiglioni was one of Italy's most influential 20th-century thinkers. This is the studio where he worked until his death in 2002, and the tours vividly illuminate his intelligent but playful creative process. Details abound; scale models of his Hilly sofa decorate a drawing table and a host of inspirational objects from joke glasses to bicycle seats await discovery. (☏02 805 36 06; www.achillecastiglioni.it; Piazza Castello 27; adult/reduced €8/6.50; ⊙tours hourly 10am-6pm Tue-Sun; ⓜCadorna)

Stazione Centrale TRAIN STATION

3 ⊙ Map p74, H1

Annually, nearly 100 million people pass through these hulking portals onto train platforms beneath a cinematic cylindrical glass roof. Begun in 1912 but realised between 1925 and 1931, the extraordinary design is flush with the nationalist fervour that marked Mussolini's rule. Most of the Fascist symbolism was removed or obscured, but the Deco-tinged neo-Babylonian architecture can hardly hide its intent. (Piazza Duca d'Aosta; ⓜCentrale FS)

Torre Pirelli LANDMARK

4 ⊙ Map p74, H2

Construction began in 1956 on Milan's tallest *grattacielo* (skyscraper). The 32-storey Pirelli Tower sits on the site of the company's 19th-century factory, symbolically bookending Italy's industrial heyday. The smooth tapered sides of Gio Ponti's modernist icon form the shape of a diamond, his oft-used graphic trademark. (Piazza Duca d'Aosta 3; ⓜCentrale FS)

Eating

10 Corso Como Café RESTAURANT, CAFE €€€

5 Map p74, E2

A picture-perfect courtyard draped in greenery awaits at Corso Como. Sit pretty in the graphic black-and-

Living (p85)

white chairs and enjoy goblets of fruit smoothie, crisp vegetable crudités and plump grilled shrimp. Plus it offers the ultimate in afternoon tea: your choice of caviar and blinis (from €55) and a pot of Mariage Frères tea. The circular bar inside is a great place for *aperitivo*, too. (📞02 2901 3581; www.10corsocomo.it; Corso Como 10; meals €35-60; ⏰12.30pm-midnight Mon-Fri, 11.30am-1.30am Sat & Sun; ❄; Ⓜ Garibaldi)

Iyo
JAPANESE €€

 Map p74, A1

Friendly staff serve great quality sashimi, *ponzu*-marinated *carpaccios* and a full range of rolls at this elegant Japanese restaurant. There's also a host of other standards from *gyoza*

(dumplings) to soba and teppan-yaki and a decent vegetarian selection. (📞02 4547 6898; www.iyo.it; Via Piero della Francesca 74; meals €30-50; ⏰noon-2.45pm & 7.30-11.45pm Tue-Sun; ❄ 🍴; 🚋1, 12)

Nisida
PIZZERIA €€

7 ✕ Map p74, E1

Nisida is renowned for its Sunday brunch antipasti. Five groaning tables support endless plates of *friarelli* (wild broccoli), smoked aubergine, raw seafood, prociutto and so it goes on. Wood-fired pizza comes thick and fast from the oven and the dessert menu features *sfogliatelle frolle* (puff pastry stuffed with ricotta, candied fruit and cinnamon), which come direct from Naples. (📞02 9737 8447;

www.nisidaverace.it; Via P Lambertenghi 19; meals €24-35; ⏱noon-3pm & 7-11.30pm Mon-Fri, dinner Sun; ❄; Ⓜ Garibaldi)

La Cantina di Manuela   ITALIAN €€

 8   Map p74, B2

This Sempione branch of the well-known *enoteca* chain has a lovely light dining room and charming staff. (Also at Via Carlo Poerio 3.) (✆02 345 20 34; www.lacantinadimanuela.it; Via Giulio Cesare Procaccini 41; meals €30-40; ⏱noon-3pm & 6pm-1am Mon-Sat; 🚋29, 30, 33)

Lyr   LEBANESE €€

 9   Map p74, B2

Like Milan, Beirut knows a thing or two about OTT style, and the chandeliers and Louis chairs make this a rather special place to feast on an authentic meze of *fattoush* (parsley and toasted bread salad), fish *kibbeh*

(dumplings), *foul moudammes* (fava beans) and grilled beef skewers. (✆02 3361 2490; www.restaurant-lyr.com; Corso Sempione 48; meals €30-35; ⏱6pm-midnight daily, noon-2.30pm Fri & Sun; ❄✎; 🚋1, 29, 30)

Trattoria degli Orti   ITALIAN €€

 10   Map p74, B2

The menu is just a formality; dishes here come along without prior consultation. Get ready for platters of gratined mussels, sardines *in saôr* (a sweet-and-sour onion jam), whitebait fritters, anchovy-stuffed zucchini flowers, homemade fish ravioli and crispy fried octopus. The lunchtime crowd of silver-haired, ties-off businessmen doesn't seem in the usual hurry to get back to work. (✆02 3310 1800; www.trattoriadegliorti.it; Via Monviso 13; meals €30-40; ⏱7.30-10.30pm Mon-Sat; 🚋12, 14)

Understand
Fiera Milano
- - - - - - - -

Milan's two fairgrounds (*fiera*) play host to an endless round of trade fairs as well as the biannual fashion blockbusters. Massimiliano Fuksas' brilliantly engineered Fiera Milano exhibition space was built on the Agip oil refinery in Rho-Pero, around 40 minutes out of town by metro. In action since 2006, its billowing glass-and-steel sail floats over 1.4km of halls, capable of holding up to half a million visitors. The city's historical fairgrounds just northwest of Parco Sempione are the site of the CityLife redevelopment, but smaller fairs are still held at the remaining pavilions, known as Fiera Milano City.

The most high-profile fair is the Furniture Fair (Salone Internazionale del Mobile) held annually in April. It attracts around 300,000 visitors and creates city-wide mayhem. For travellers, proximity to the red (M1) metro line is really all that matters. If you're coming to town, be sure to book ahead for everything.

Drinking

Living BAR

11 Map p74, C3

Living has one of the city's prettiest settings, with a corner position and floor-to-ceiling windows overlooking the Arco della Pace. The bounteous *aperitivo* spread and expertly mixed cocktails draw crowds of smart-casual 20- and 30-somethings. (02 3310 0824; www .livingmilano.com; Piazza Sempione 2; 8am-2am Mon-Fri, 9am-2am Sat & Sun; Moscova)

Milano BAR

12 Map p74, B2

This popular bar shares owners with Roialto. It's smaller and starker than Roialto (though still huge by any other standards), but bears many of its trademarks. There's vintage '60s and '70s furniture in black, white and orange, stacks (literally) of interiors magazines and the 'too much is never enough' *aperitivo,* with many items cooked to order. (02 3493 0819; http://roialtogroup.it/milano; Via Procaccini 37; 6pm-2am Tue-Sat; 29, 30, 33)

Roialto BAR, CLUB

13 Map p74, A1

This high-ceilinged former market is strewn with '70s sofas and bright young things. The *aperitivo* here is famously unstinting, though the international hotel buffet breakfast vibe conjured by uniformed staff at twee stations (doling out oysters, artisan cheeses and whatever you damn well want) can hardly be cool, can it? (02 3493 6616; http://roialtogroup.it; Via Piero della Francesca 55; 6pm-2am Tue-Sun; 1, 14, 19, 33)

Cantine Isola ENOTECA

14 Map p74, C2

Only octogenarians make use of the table in the back – everyone else hovers near the beautiful old bar, balancing plates of *bruschetta* and holding glasses at the ready for their selection of wines from 400 exceptional vintners. (02 331 52 49; Via Paolo Sarpi 30; 8.30am-9.30pm Tue-Sun; Garibaldi)

Frida BAR

15 Map p74, E1

The jumble of tables in the heated courtyard and comfy couches inside make it easy to bond over beer or regional wine with an arty crowd. The *aperitivo* spread is continuously replenished and sports plenty of veggie dishes. No pretensions, no entourages, just good music, good value and good times. (02 68 02 60; www.fridaisola.it; Via Pollaiuolo 3; bar 6pm-2am Mon-Sun, restaurant 12.30-3pm Mon-Fri, noon-4pm Sun; Zara, Garibaldi)

Nordest Caffé BAR, CAFE

16 Map p74, F1

So laid-back you might have trouble getting served, this sunny cafe-bar invites long, lazy afternoons. The young local crowd has that down to an art, especially for Sunday brunch from noon, when the live jazz begins. (02 6900 1910; www.nordestcaffe.it; Via Borsieri 35; 8am-1.30pm Mon, 8am-midnight Tue-Sat, 8.30am-10pm Sun; ; Garibaldi, Zara)

Old Fashion Café

BAR, CLUB

17 Map p74, C4

Wade through the furiously texting *figli di papa* (rich brats) and make it past the bouncers, and you'll be rewarded with an expansive outdoor bar that sits in the shadow of the Triennale and Parco Sempione trees. But with the *aperitivo* queues and an ultracommercial soundtrack, you'll need youth or supernatural stamina to make it to sunrise. (02 805 62 31;

www.oldfashion.it; Viale Emilio Alemagna 6; 10pm-4.30am; Cadorna)

Il Gattopardo

BAR, CLUB

18 Map p74, A2

This gorgeous Champagne-coloured space in a deconsecrated church is filled with flickering candles and Baroque-style furniture. Gattopardo's clientele is equally aesthetically blessed. (02 3453 7699; www.ilgattopardocafe.it; Via Piero della Francesca 47; 6pm-5am Tue-Sun; Lotto, 1, 14, 19, 33)

Hollywood

CLUB

19 Map p74, E2

This is the club frequented by footballers and supermodels, and those

Fashion, 10 Corso Como (p89)

that come to gawk at them. If you make it in, you might see the next scandal in the making, or you might wonder what the fuss is about. (📞02 33556 53814; www.discotecahollywood.com; Corso Como 15; ⏱10.30pm-2am Tue-Sun; Ⓜ Garibaldi)

Entertainment

Alcatraz   CLUB

20 ⭐ Map p74, D1

Founded by Italian rockstar Vasco Rossi, Alcatraz is now a multifunctional venue for live concerts, DJ sets, fashion shows and a weekly dance club. The 1800-sq-metre former garage space rocks to the sound of latino, house and revival on Friday, and classic rock'n'roll on Saturday. Check the website for featured gigs. (📞02 6901 6352; www.alcatrazmilano.com; Via Valtellina 25; ⏱11pm-4am Fri & Sat Sep-Jun; 🚊3, 4, 7, 11, 🚍70)

Blue Note   JAZZ CLUB

21 ⭐ Map p74, F1

Top-class jazz acts perform here from around the world; get tickets by phone, online or at the door from 7.30pm. It also does a popular easy-listening Sunday brunch (€35 or €55 for two adults and two children). (📞02 6901 6888; www.bluenotemilano.com; Via Borsieri 37; tickets €25-30; ⏱Tue-Sun Sep-Jul; Ⓜ Zara, Garibaldi)

🔍 Local Life
Chinatown

Milan's **Chinatown** (Map p74, D2) is centred on Via Paolo Sarpi and Via Donato Bramante. The Chinese community has deep roots in the city, with families that settled here in the 1920s and '30s.

While Milan likes to think of itself as Italy's most multicultural city, casual racism or the flip fetishism of fashionland is a common response to questions of ethnic identity. Tensions exploded in 2007, following police harassment of local textile workers, and a demonstration that turned into a riot was met with a flurry of anti-immigration sentiment. But hard work and harmony is the usual order of the day.

The area is a good shopping alternative, too. Pick up bargain clothing, leatherwear and electrical goods, as well as Asian produce.

Nuova Idea   CLUB

22 ⭐ Map p74, F1

Go club-hopping without leaving this many-splendoured nightlife theme park, one of Milan's premier gay clubs since 1975. One room features ballroom dancing, the next cages with greased-up gogo dancers. At the centre of it all, celebrated transvestites put Fashion Week runway shows to shame. (📞02 6900 7859; www.lanuovaidea.com; Via Gaetano De Castillia 30; admission €10 Fri & Sun, €18 Sat, Thu free with drink; ⏱10.30pm-3am Thu-Sun; Ⓜ Gioia)

Understand
Living by Design

From the cup that holds your morning espresso to the bedside light you click off before you go to sleep, there's a designer responsible – and almost everyone in Milan knows their name.

Design Roots
The roots of Italian design can be found in 1930s Milan, with the opening of the Triennale, the founding of *Domus* and *Casabella* design magazines, Rinascente's visionary commissions and the development of the Fiera as a modern marketplace. As large-scale industrial design came late to Italy, a decorative joy persisted, despite the onslaught of modernist rigour.

Philosopher-Architects
With the end of WWII, Milanese authorities focused on rebuilding. Luckily for them the 1930s and '40s spawned a school of architect-philosophers (Giò Ponti, Piero Fornasetti, Enzo Mari, the Castiglioni brothers, Mario Bellini, Gae Aulenti and Ettore Sottsass) concerned with redesigning the city for a new age. They were imbued with modernist optimism, believing that designers and architects sat between art and society, and that they should create objects and spaces with both function and beauty.

From Producer...
Milan's designers also benefitted from a unique proximity to a highly skilled artisanal workforce spread across the northern Lombard district of Brianza. Populated by many small craft business, engaged in textiles (the silk mills of Como), carpentry (the production of furniture and musical instruments), leatherwork and metalwork, the Brianza craftsmen provided a technical workforce who could make their modernist dreams come true.

...To Market
While Brianza's production houses remained true to the craft aspect of their work, they were able to move towards modern sales and production techniques via Milan's Fiera. With the opening of the trade Triennale in 1933, Milan established a forum for designers, architects and manufacturers to come together. This connection between producer and marketplace established a happy symbiosis between creativity and commercialism that ultimately fine-tuned Italian design to achieve the modernist ideal of creating desirable, useful objects.

Anteospazio Cinema CINEMA

23 ⭐ Map p74, E3

On rainy Mondays take your pick of three screens showing original-language films, from classics to indies, then loiter in the bookshop, restaurant and exhibition space. (☎02 659 77 32; www.spaziocinema.info; Via Milazzo 9; Ⓜ Moscova)

Shopping

10 Corso Como FASHION

(5) 🔒 Map p74, E2

Carla Sozzani's consistently clever selection of highly desirable things really does make 10 Corso Como Milan's most thrilling shopping experience. Upstairs there is an equally browsable bookshop and a large music department. (☎02 2900 2674; www.10corsocomo.com; Corso Como 10; ⏱10.30am-7.30pm Tue & Fri-Sun, to 9pm Wed & Thu, 3.30-7.30pm Mon; Ⓜ Garibaldi)

Vintage Delirium VINTAGE

24 🔒 Map p74, E5

Franco Jacassi's multilevel shop stocks pristine vintage woollens, 1930s evening wear (Chanel, Dior, Balenciaga and Vionnet), belts, buckles, bags and Neapolitan silk ties from the 1960s. (☎02 8646 2076; www.vintagedeliriumfj.com; Via Sacchi 3; ⏱10am-1pm & 2-7pm Mon-Fri Sep-Jul; Ⓜ Cairoli)

10 Corso Como Outlet FASHION

25 🔒 Map p74, E2

At the back of a sunny courtyard, you'll find a surprisingly serene outlet store. There are genuine bargains on big names such as Marni, Prada and Comme, and even better discounts on quirkier pieces like Stephen Jones hats. Menswear is particularly strong. (☎02 2900 2674; www.10corsocomo.com; Via Tazzoli 3; ⏱1-7pm Fri, 11am-7pm Sat & Sun; Ⓜ Garibaldi, 🚃3, 4)

Monica Castiglioni JEWELLERY

26 🔒 Map p74, E1

Located in Isola, Monica's studio turns out organic, industrial-style jewellery in bronze, silver and gold. Deeply rooted in Milan's modernist traditions, these are statement pieces and well priced for the workmanship. (☎02 8723 7979; www.monicacastiglioni.com; Via Pastrengo 4; ⏱11am-8pm Thu-Sat; Ⓜ Garibaldi)

Officina Slowear FASHION

27 🔒 Map p74, D3

Slowear takes its cue from the Slow Food philosophy and markets a stable of labels (Incotex, Zanone) that all fit a wearable, reasonably timeless and beautifully tactile bill. Perfect for scouting a new office wardrobe. (☎02 3310 0774; www.slowear.com; Viale Elvezia 6; ⏱10am-7pm Mon-Sat; Ⓜ Moscova)

Explore

Corso Magenta & Sant'Ambrogio

It's usually Leonardo da Vinci's *Cenacolo,* or the basilica of Sant'Ambrogio that draws visitors here, but there's an equal mix of the sacred and the secular in these leafy streets. Piazza Cordusio is the home of high finance, hence the bars full of young bankers, while to the south Bramante's cloisters ring with the chatter of students at the sprawling Università Cattolica.

The Sights in a Day

☀️ A coffee and cornetto at **Biffi** (p99) marks the start of the day. Then, fully fortified, head to the **science museum** (p94) for a morning marvelling at models of Leonardo's machines alongside fascinating exhibits in music, astrology, horology, metallurgy, ballistics, aeronautics and transport.

☀️ Then grab a quick panino and beer with locals at **Bar Magenta** (p99) and toss a coin for your next stop; the golden sky and Saint Ambrogio's tomb at Milan's most important **basilica** (p97) or Bernardino Luini's heavenly frescoes at the **Chiesa di San Maurizio** (p97) and a quick lesson in the city's history at the adjoining **Archaeological Museum** (p98).

🌙 With your pre-booked evening ticket to **Il Cenacolo** (p93) tucked safely in your pocket, stop for a leisurely glass of wine and platter of *aperitivo* goodies at **Per Bacco** (p100), before finishing the day gazing on Leonardo da Vinci's masterful mural in the refectory of Santa Maria delle Grazie. A guided tour or audio guide is well worth the investment.

 Top Sights

Basilica di Santa Maria delle Grazie (p92)

Museo Nazionale della Scienza e della Tecnologia (p94)

 Best of Milan

History
Basilica di Sant'Ambrogio (p97)

Civico Museo Archeologico (p98)

Art
Il Cenacolo (p93)

Chiesa di San Maurizio (p97)

Museums
Museo Nazionale della Scienza e della Tecnologia (p94)

Shopping
Pupi Solari (p101)

Calé Fragranza d'Autore (p100)

Getting There

Ⓜ **Metro** Use Sant'Ambrogio on MM2 (green line) for Sant'Ambrogio. Cadorna (MM1) is best for *Il Cenacolo,* the archaeological museum and San Maurizio; use the Conciliazione, Pagano and Wagner stops for Corso Magenta and Corso Vercelli.

Top Sights
Basilica di Santa Maria delle Grazie

Milan's most famous painting, Leonardo da Vinci's *Il Cenacolo* (The Last Supper), is hidden away on a wall of the refectory adjoining the basilica of Santa Maria delle Grazie. Depicting Christ and his disciples at the dramatic moment when Christ reveals he is aware of the betrayal afoot, it is a masterful psychological study and one of the world's most iconic images.

Map p96, C2

Piazza Santa Maria delle Grazie 2

ⓂCadorna

Il Cenacolo

Don't Miss

Il Cenacolo

When Leonardo was at work on **Il Cenacolo** (☎02 9280 0360; www.cenacolovinciano.net; Piazza Santa Maria delle Grazie 2; adult/reduced €6.50/3.25, plus €1.50 booking fee; ⏰8.15am-7pm Mon-Sat; Ⓜ Cadorna), a star-struck monk noted that he would sometimes arrive in the morning, stare at yesterday's effort, then promptly call it quits for the day. Your visit too will be similarly brief (15 minutes to be exact) but the baggage of a thousand dodgy reproductions are quickly shed once face to face with the luminous work itself. Da Vinci's experimental techniques and years of wear have left the mural fragile, but its condition does nothing to lessen the astonishing beauty and enthralling psychological drama before you.

The Basilica

Any visit to *Il Cenacolo* should be accompanied by a tour of Santa Maria delle Grazie, a Unesco World Heritage site. Designed by Guiniforte Solari with later additions by Bramante, it encapsulates the magnificence of the court of Ludovico 'il Moro' Sforza and Beatrice d'Este. Articulated in fine brickwork and terracotta, the building is robust but fanciful, its apse topped by Bramante's cupola and its interior lined with frescoes.

Codex Atlanticus

The *Codex Atlanticus* is the largest collection of da Vinci's drawings in the world. More than 1700 of them were gathered by sculptor Pompeo Leoni, enough to make up 12 volumes so heavy they threatened the preservation of the drawings themselves. The sheets have now been unbound and are displayed in softly lit glass cases in Bramante's sacristy.

☑ Top Tips

▶ Reservations to view *Il Cenacolo* must be made weeks, if not months, in advance. Or you can take a city tour that includes a visit.

▶ Once booked, you'll be allotted a strict visiting time. If you're late, your ticket will be resold.

▶ Multilingual guided tours (€3.25) are on offer and also need to be reserved in advance.

▶ Drawings from da Vinci's *Codex Atlanticus* are displayed in the Sagrestia Bramantesca.

✕ Take a Break

Enjoy an espresso and slice of artisanal panettone beneath the Murano chandeliers of Art-Deco Biffi (p99).

Follow Leonardo's divine dining experience with an eight-course cheese and salami tasting at Boccondivino (p98).

Top Sights
Museo Nazionale della Scienza e della Tecnologia

Kids, would-be inventors and geeks will go goggle-eyed at Milan's impressive museum of science and technology, the largest of its kind in Italy. It is a fitting tribute to arch-inventor Leonardo da Vinci, who did much of his finest work in the city. The 16th-century monastery, where it is housed, features a collection of more than 10,000 items, including models based on da Vinci's engineering sketches, halls devoted to the sciences of physics, astronomy and horology, and outdoor hangars housing steam trains, planes and full-sized galleons.

Map p96, C3

www.museoscienza.org

Via San Vittore 21

adult/reduced €10/7, submarine tour €8

9.30am-5pm Tue-Fri, to 6.30pm Sat & Sun

M Sant'Ambrogio

Locomotive, Museo Nazionale della Scienza e della Tecnologia

Don't Miss

Leonardo da Vinci Gallery
In 1481 Leonardo da Vinci wrote to Ludovico Sforza applying for a position at court. He had been recommended as a musician, but he promoted himself as an engineer, promising the duke he could build him all manner of war machines, improve the castle fortifications, tinker with the city's canal system and, if there was nothing else to do, he could always paint the Duke's mistresses. He filled dozens of notebooks with sketches, models of which line the Leonardo gallery.

Air & Transport Pavilion
This pavilion wows the crowds with full-sized ships and planes suspended from the rafters. Exquisitely crafted 17th- and 18th-century models of sailing ships sit beside the real thing, including the brigantine schooner *Ebe* and the command bridge of the *Conte Biancamano*, a transatlantic oceanliner. You can also wander through its Banquet Hall and 1st-class cabins.

Enrico Toti Submarine
One of the museum's biggest draws is the *Enrico Toti* submarine, which sits incongruously in its back yard. The first submarine constructed in Italy after WWII, it was launched in 1967 primarily as a deterrent against the nuclear-propelled torpedo launchers the Soviet Union was sending forth. Take the guided tour for a first-hand experience of its claustrophic quarters.

☑ Top Tips

▶ The museum has a weekend program of interactive laboratories and experiments for children.

▶ Give yourself at least half a day to explore the museum, which consists of three main areas: the three-storey monastery, with collections and i.labs; the Air & Sea Transport Pavilion, full of boats and planes; and the Rail Transport Pavilion.

▶ You can only board the *Enrico Toti* submarine on a tour, which should be booked at the information desk.

▶ There's an on-site bar and canteen if the kids (or you) need to refuel.

✕ Take a Break

Stop for coffee, beer or a panini at historical Bar Magenta (p99) and enjoy its lovely Liberty decor.

For delicious Sardinian dishes and a family-friendly welcome, head east to Osteria al Molo 13 (p98).

Sights

Basilica di Sant'Ambrogio CHURCH

1 ◉ Map p96, D3

St Ambrose, Milan's patron saint and superstar bishop, is buried in the crypt of the Basilica di Sant'Ambrogio, which he founded in AD 379. It's a fitting legacy, built and rebuilt with a purposeful simplicity that is truly uplifting. Shimmering altar mosaics and an AD 835 gilt altarpiece light up the shadowy vaulted interior. (☎02 8645 0895; www.basilicasantambrogio.it; Piazza Sant'Ambrogio 15; ◷10am-noon & 2.30-6pm Mon-Sat, 3-5pm Sun; Ⓜ Sant'Ambrogio)

Chiesa di San Maurizio CHAPEL, CONVENT

2 ◉ Map p96, E2

The 16th-century royal chapel and convent of San Maurizio is Milan's hidden crown jewel. Every inch is covered in Bernardino Luini's frescoes, many immortalising Ippolita Sforza and her family. Duck through the arch to the left of the altar and into the secluded convent hall where blissful martyred women saints bear their tribulations serenely – note Santa Agata casually carrying her breasts on a platter. (Corso Magenta 15; ◷9am-noon & 2-5.30pm Tue-Sun; Ⓜ Cadorna)

Bernardino Luini fresco, Chiesa di San Maurizio

Civico Museo Archeologico　ARCHAEOLOGICAL MUSEUM

3 　◉ 　Map p96, D2

Adjoining San Maurizio is the 9th-century Monastero Maggiore, once the most important Benedictine convent in the city and now the archaeological museum. Accessed via a cloister featuring fragments of the city's Roman walls and through the 3rd-century frescoed Ansperto Tower, it provides a glimpse of Roman Mediolanum with collections of Etruscan, Greek, Roman, Gothic and Lombard artefacts. (☑02 8844 5208; www.comune.milano.it/musei emostre; Corso Magenta 15; adult/reduced €2/1; ◷9am-5.30pm Tue-Sun; Ⓜ Cadorna)

🔍 Local Life
San Siro

San Siro Stadium wasn't designed to hold the entire population of Milan, but on a Sunday afternoon amid 85,000 football-mad fans, it can certainly feel like it. The city's two clubs, AC Milan and FC Internazionale Milano (aka Inter), play on alternate weeks between October and May. The crosstown derby, known as the Derby della Madonnina, is one of the greatest rivalries in the world. Serie A fans can head for the **Museo Inter e Milan** (☑02 404 2432 Via Piccolomini 5, Gate 21; www.sansiro.net; museum & tour adult/reduced €13/10; ◷10am-6pm) for nonstop screenings of matches, memorabilia and trophies galore.

Habits Culti Spa　SPA

4 　◉ 　Map p96, A2

Culti's ethno-sacred aesthetic lives large at this sensual spa. Treatments don't come cheap (€80 for a basic manicure), but this is no corner nail bar. Stone, wood and water are highlighted in the decor and treatments utilise flowers, salts and mud. (☑02 4851 7588; www.culti.it; Via Angelo Mauri 5; baths per couple €110, hammam €90-150; ◷11am-10pm Mon-Sat, 10am-8pm Sun; Ⓜ Conciliazione)

Eating

Osteria al Molo 13　SARDINIAN €€

5 　✕ 　Map p96, A2

Decorated in bright colours reminiscent of the south, Pino and Max Zucca's eatery brings a taste of Sardinia to Milan. Their passion is present in each mouthful of *carpaccio* (finely sliced raw beef) and bottarga (grey mullet roe). Original artworks and chequered tablecloths make you feel like you're at Baia Chia more than central Milan. (☑02 404 27 43; www.trattoriamolo.it; Via Pietro Paolo Rubens 13; meals €30-45; ◷noon-3pm & 7-11.30pm Tue-Sat, 7-11.30pm Mon; ❄ ; Ⓜ De Angeli)

Boccondivino　ENOTECA €€€

6 　✕ 　Map p96, D2

The 'divine mouthful' that *boccondivino* alludes to actually runs to eight tasting courses, starting with *prosecco* and pâté, followed by ham and salami (sweet and smoked), a *primi* of tortel-loni, gnocchi or risotto, groaning trol-leys of cheese and finally sorbet and *biscotti*. Each course is paired with a matching wine. (☑02 86 60 40; www.boc condivino.com; Via Carducci 17; meals €50-70; ☺8pm-midnight Mon-Sat; ✷; Ⓜ Cadorna)

Biffi Pasticceria
PASTICCERIA €

 7 Map p96, B2

Proud keepers of a *panetùn* (panet-tone) recipe that once pleased Pope Pius X, Biffi has changed little since its 1847 opening. With its polished walnut bar, marble counters and Mu-rano chandeliers, its air of old-world elegance continues to attract *borghese*, who come to gossip over cream cakes and cocktails. (☑02 4800 6702; www.biffi pasticceria.it; Corso Magenta 87; pastries €2.50; ☺7am-8.30pm; ✷; ➽; Ⓜ Conciliazione)

La Collina d'Oro
ASIAN €€

 8 Map p96, A2

A bright modern interior sets the scene for a pan-Asian menu that has not only Chinese and Japanese staples but also some Southeast Asian dishes. (☑02 404 31 48; www.lacollinadoro.com; Via Rubens 24; meals €25-35; ☺11am-3pm & 6.30-11.30pm Tue-Sun; Ⓜ De Angeli)

Zero
JAPANESE €€€

 9 Map p96, B2

Zero's dramatically designed space puts the spotlight on the kitchen, which prepares traditional sashimi but also a variety of creative raw

Milan's Best Gelati

Despite its out-of-the-way loca-tion, **Gelateria Marghera** (☑02 46 86 41; Via Marghera 33) has the repu-tation as the city's best ice-cream parlour – which means concerted queuing can be required to get in the door. Its range of ice-cream cakes and *liquorini* (layered gelati or sorbet with fruit or nut toppings and, you guessed it, liquor) are worth the wait. Their best-selling flavour? Pistachio.

Marginally less busy is **Shock-olat** (☑02 4810 0597; Via Boccaccio 9; ☺7.30am-1am), where variations play on the chocolate theme including milk, dark, white, chilli, chocolate-hazelnut and cinnamon.

and rare dishes. Japanese technique dominates, while the menu flirts with Italian flavours and ingredients (in-cluding a *carpaccio*-style Angus beef). (☑02 4547 4733; www.zeromagenta.it; Corso Magenta 87; meals €60-80; ☺restaurant 7.30pm-midnight Mon-Sat, shop 12.30-2.30pm Tue-Sat; ➽; Ⓜ Conciliazione)

Drinking

Bar Magenta
BAR

 10 Map p96, D2

Grab a seat in this historical bar and let Milan come to you. Drift in during the day for espresso, sandwiches and beer, or join the students during

early evening for wine from a tap.
(📞02 805 38 08; www.bar-magenta.it; Via
Giosué Carducci 13; ⏰8am-2am; Ⓜ Cadorna)

Enoteca Per Bacco
ENOTECA

11 Map p96, D2

Laid-back Per Bacco is a perfect pit
stop for an early evening glass of wine
and a *caprese* salad or selection of
crostini. There's a good selection of
wines by the glass (€5) from a cellar
of 400 labels, and from time to time
there are themed tastings. (📞02 8645
2009; Via Giosuè Carducci 9; ⏰noon-2.30pm
& 7pm-midnight Tue-Sun; Ⓜ Cadorna)

Noy
BAR

12 Map p96, A2

With its uptight-housewife-gets-her-
groove-back-at-the-ashram decor, only
the corrugated roof gives this former
garage's past life away. A plate of the
fresh and generous *aperitivo* spread
starts the night right. Cocktails, perfect for retoxing after a wellness treat-
ment at Habits Culti spa next door,
come next. (📞02 4811 0375; www.noymi
lano.com; Via Soresina 4; ⏰11.30am-midnight
Tue-Sun, to 1am Fri & Sat; Ⓜ Conciliazione)

Shopping

Agua del Carmen
FASHION

13 Map p96, E4

Fornasetti faces appear to signal their
approval of the great mix of ultrawear-
able clothes, shoes and bags. Orla
Kiely totes, Pedro Garcia flats and

Sylvie Quartara flip-flops are sensible
(and sensibly priced) but have eye-
candy appeal, too. (📞02 8941 5363;
www.aguadelcarmen.it; Via Cesare Correnti
23; ⏰3-7.30pm Mon, 10am-7.30pm Tue-Sat;
Ⓜ Sant'Ambrogio)

Calé Fragranza d'Autore
PERFUMERY

14 Map p96, E2

Since 1955 artistic perfumery Calé has
been a creator and purveyor of artisan
fragrances, featuring cult names such
as Parfums d'Orsay, Humietski &
Graef, Rigaud and Truefitt & Hill. The
clean aromatic notes of its own-brand
perfume embody the minimal Milanese style. (📞02 8050 9449; www
.cale.it; Via Santa Maria alla Porta 5; ⏰3-7pm
Mon, 10am-7pm Tue-Sat; Ⓜ Cairoli)

Henry Beguelin
FASHION

15 Map p96, D4

Softly unconstructed coats, strappy
sandals and earthy decorated bags
are handmade using leather that's
been tanned and dyed using traditional techniques. The haute-hippie
look is also carried through to linen
separates for summer. (📞02 7200 0959;
www.henrybeguelin.it; Via Caminadella 7;
⏰3-7.30pm Mon, 10.30am-7.30pm Tue-Sun;
Ⓜ Sant'Ambrogio)

Libreria degli Atellani
BOOKSHOP

16 Map p96, C2

Opposite the church of Santa Maria
delle Grazie, Atellani offers a vast
selection of novels and magazines

Spazio Rossana Orlandi

in English. The building, Casa degli
Atellani, was previously a palazzo
where Leonardo lived while working
on *Il Cenacolo,* and was remodelled by
modernist architect Piero Portaluppi.
(☎02 481 61 50; www.atellani.it; Corso Magenta 65; ⊗7.30am-7.30pm; Ⓜ Cadorna)

Pupi Solari
FASHION

17 🔒 Map p96, B1

Milanese from a certain kind of
family will recall regular Pupi Solari
visits for shoe fittings and picking out
exquisitely decorated party dresses or
tweed jackets just like daddy's. The
wonderfully lavish window displays
still delight; there's now a women's
department and, in the same square,
a menswear branch, Host. (☎02 46

33 25; www.pupisolari.it; Piazza Tommaseo
2; ⊗10am-7.30pm Tue-Sat; Ⓜ Conciliazione,
🚎 29, 30)

Spazio Rossana
Orlandi
HOME & GARDEN, DESIGN

18 🔒 Map p96, B3

Finding this iconic interior design
studio, which is installed in a former
tie factory in the Magenta district,
is a challenge in itself. Once inside,
though, you'll find it hard to leave
this dream-like treasure trove stacked
with vintage and contemporary
limited-edition pieces from young and
upcoming artists. (☎02 467 44 71; www
.rossanaorlandi.com; Via Matteo Bandello 14;
⊗3.30-7.30pm Mon, 10am-7.30pm Tue-Fri;
Ⓜ Conciliazione)

Explore

Navigli &
Porta Romana

Corso di Porta Romana runs southeast from the centre past the Universitá Statale and on to Porta Romana, one of the city gates originally built by Barbarossa in the 12th century, on the ancient road to Rome. Along with Navigli, the area is home to the best bars, clubs and live-music venues, which nestle between grand *palazzi* and along the edges of the city's canals.

The Sights in a Day

 Brunch on the back patio of **El Brellin** (p105) is the way to start the day. It's situated on picturesque Vicolo dei Lavandai, where women once brought their laundry to scrub against the flat stones. Afterwards, consider hopping aboard a **Navigli Lombardi** (p105) barge for a one-hour tour of the canals. Longer day tours are also available, and include lunch and afternoon bike hire.

 For those returning early, consider lunch at Slow Food–recommended **Le Vigne** (p109), and then browse the funky shops along Ripa di Porta Ticinese. As the afternoon wanes, make your way up to the **San Lorenzo columns** (p108) for ice cream or *aperitivo* with the rest of the city, who appear to be camped out in the piazza. **Cantina della Vetra** (p110), with views over the piazza, is known for its wine cellar.

The evening is just getting going about now, so move on to drinks at retro **Cuore** (p110) or **Refeel** (p111). Then around 11pm check into one of Porta Romana's thumping clubs. **Magazzini Generali** (p112) and **Plastic** (p111) draw the biggest crowds.

For a local's day on the canals, see p104.

Local Life
Life on the Canals (p104)

Best of Milan

Eating
Sadler (p110)

Sushi Koboo (p110)

Gattullo (p110)

Drinking
Le Trottoir (p111)

Lacerba (p111)

Nightlife
Plastic (p111)

Magazzini Generali (p112)

Shopping
Frip (p113)

Superfly (p105)

Getting There

M Metro Missori, Crocetta, Porta Romana and Lodi on MM3 (yellow line) give good access to the Porta Romana neighbourhood. Porta Genova on MM2 is best for bars on Via Vigevano and the Naviglio Grande canal.

Tram Use tram 3 for the shops along Corso di Porta Ticinese, Piazza XXIV Maggio and the Alzaia Naviglio Pavese canal.

Local Life
Life on the Canals

The Navigli neighbourhood is named after its most identifiable feature – the canals. Designed as the motorways of medieval Milan, they powered the city's fortunes until the railroads, WWII bombs and neglect brought about their closure in the 1970s. These days they provide a scenic backdrop to the bookshops, boutiques and bars that make this Milan's most kicking Bohemian 'burb.

❶ Neighbourhood Markets
Overlooking the Darsena is the **Mercato Comunale** (Piazza XXIV Maggio; ☉Mon-Sat), the city's main covered market, selling fresh produce and fish. Come the last Sunday of the month and you'll find the **Mercatore Antiquario di Navigli** set up along a 2km stretch of the Navigli Grande. With more than 400 well-vetted antique and secondhand traders, it provides hours of treasure-hunting pleasure.

❷ Brunch

Housed in an 18th-century laundry, **El Brellin** (☎02 5810 1351; www.brellin.com; cnr Vicolo dei Lavandai 14 & Alzaia Naviglio Grande 14; meals €40-45; ☺Mon-Sat) is a romantic spot. The Sunday brunch buffet is laden with cured meats, scrambled eggs, smoked salmon, and homemade desserts including the Milanese in-joke, biscuit-filled chocolate 'salami'.

❸ Boat Tours

Canals were the autostrade of medieval Milan, transporting lumber, marble, salt, oil and wine. The largest, Navigli Grande, grew from an irrigation ditch to become one of the city's busiest thoroughfares. You can take a boat tour with **Navigli Lombardi** (☎02 9227 3118; www.navigliilombardi.it; Alzaia Naviglio Grande 4, Porta Genova area near Scodellino bridge; adult/reduced €12/10; ☺Apr-Sep; Ⓜ Porta Genova, 🚊3), for views of the churches and villas that line its banks.

❹ Aperitivo

On weekend and summer evenings, Milanese come for Navigli's *aperitivo* scene. Almost every bar along the Navigli Grande offers an *aperitivo* buffet. Some, like **El Brellin** (see No 2, left) , while grungy **Plat du Jour** (☎02 832 1823; Via Vigevano 2; ☺Tue-Sun; Ⓜ Porta Genova, 🚊2, 3) overflows with beer-touting 20-somethings. Corks start popping at about 7pm.

❺ Browsing

With its old laundries and warehouses, pretty iron bridges and low rents, Nav-igli is home to a thriving community of artists and musicians. Eclectic studios and shops line the canals, perfect for window-shopping. Highlights include **Mauro Bolognesi** (☎02 837 6028; www.maurobolognesi.com; Ripa di Porta Ticinese 47; ☺9.30am-12.30pm & 3-7pm Tue-Sat; Ⓜ Porta Genovese) with modern collectibles and furniture, **SuperGulp** (☎02 837 2216; www.supergulp.net; Ripa di Porta Ticinese 51; ☺10am-1pm & 3pm-midnight Tue-Sat, 3pm-midnight Sun, 3-8pm Mon) for comics, gadgets and posters, and **Superfly** (☎339 579 2838; www.superflyvintage.com; Ripa di Porta Ticinese 27; ☺11am-8pm Tue-Sat, 3-7pm Sun) for vintage disco diva gear.

❻ Enoteca

An alternative spot for *aperitivo* is **Bond** (☎02 5810 8375; Via Paoli 2; ☺10pm-3am Tue-Sun; Ⓜ Porta Genova), whioh ca-ters to an older, wine-drinking crowd

❼ Canal Dining

For a unique eating experience, head south along the Navigli Pavese, origi-nally created to irrigate Gian Galeazzo's hunting reserve near Pavia. Over the highway and left down Via Ascanio Sforza, you'll find **L'Osteria Grand Ho-tel** (☎02 8951 1586; www.osteriagrandhotel.it; Via Cardinale Ascanio Sforza 75; meals €35-40; ☺dinner Mon-Fri, lunch & dinner Sat & Sun), a little slice of the Lombard countryside in the city. In summer you can dine with locals beneath the wisteria-shaded patio overlooking the bocce court. Between the 600-label wine list, artisanal Alpine cheeses and regional special-ities, you'll have a hard time leaving.

A

B

C

D

1

Via Edmondo de Amicis

Largo Carrobbio

M Missori

Corso di Porta Romana

Torre Velasca

M Sant'Agostino

Via C Correnti

24

Via Stampa

Via Olmetto

Piazza San Nazaro in Brolo

12

10

Piazza Vetra

2

Basilica di San Lorenzo Maggiore

21

Corso Genova

San Lorenzo Columns

1

Via Ausonio

Via Molino delle Armi

Corso Italia

Via Santa Sofia

2

Stazione Porta Genova

Corso C Colombo

Via Gaudenzio Ferrari

Viale Gabriele Annunzio

Corso di Porta Ticinese

Basilica di Sant'Eustorgio

Via G Mercalli

M Porta Genova

Via Gorizia

Via Arena

Dugnano

3

Via S Martino

Via Burigozzo

Via Bianca di Savoia

Via Vigevano

Piazza XXIV Maggio

14

Vle Gian Galeazzo

9

Via Valenza

Ripa di Porta Ticinese

Viale Col Di Lana

8

Viale Beatrice d'Es

3

Via Angelo Fumagalli

6

Via Paoli

Alzaia Naviglio Pavese

Via Pietro Teulie

Università Bocconi

Via F Bocconi

Viale Blig

Via Giovanni Segantini

Via Giosuè Borsi

Corso San Gottardo

Via Pavia

Via Odoardo Tabacchi

Via R Sarfatti

Parco Ravizz

NAVIGLI

20

Via Conchetta

19

Via Giuseppe Meda

Via Castelbarco

Viale Toscana

4

Viale Liguria

Viale Tibaldi

Via Imperia

11

Via C Ascanio Sforza

Via Privata Alcardo

Via Giovanni Pezzotti

Via Carlo Bazzi

Via dei Fonta

Via Rimini

Via La Spezia

Via Bernardino Verro

Via Giaco

5

Famagosta M

Piazzale Francesco Carrara

Via Giovanni da Cermenate

Via Giaco Antonir

Università
le Giardino
della Guastalla

E

Ospedale
Maggiore
Policlinico

Crocetta

Via A Lamarmora

Corso di Porta Romana

13

Corso di Porta tina

Via Orti

Viale Emilio Caldara

Via A Filippetti

Viale Sabotino

15

Porta
Romana

PORTA
ROMANA

F

Via Pace

Viale Regina Margherita

Viale Lazio

Via Pier Lombardo

Via S Luttuada

Via Ludovico Muratori

7 5

Via L Papi

Via Crema

Via Mantova

G

23

Via Sciesa

Via Spartaco

Via Fogazzaro

Via Sigieri

Piazzale
Libia

Vle Cirene

Via Tiraboschi

Via Ludovico Muratori

Via Colletta
Pietro

Viale Umbria

Via Fontana

Via Cadore

4 Fondazione
Prada

Via Comelico

Via Bergamo

H

Largo
Marinai
d'Italia

16

Piazzale
F Martini

Piazza
Insubria

Via Tito Livio

1

2

3

a G Bellezza

Via Palladio

Via G Ripamonti

Via
Pietrasanta

Via G Lorenzini

Via G Romano

Viale Isonzo

Via Brembo

Lodi
TIBB

Porta
Romana

Via Leo Longanesi

Corso Lodi

Viale Isonzo

4

For reviews see

◉	Sights	p108
✖	Eating	p108
♪	Drinking	p110
✿	Entertainment	p112
🛍	Shopping	p113

Viale Ortles

Via Pasinetti

Via Barletta

18

N

0   1 km
0   0.5 miles

5

Sights

Basilica di San Lorenzo Maggiore
BASILICA

1 Map p106, C1

The touching simplicity of this early Christian basilica, with its central dome and squat towers, managed to survive a substantial reconstruction in the 16th century. The octagonal Cappella di Sant'Aquilino's 4th-century mosaic of a toga-clad Jesus holding court is also the real deal; the highly individual and seemingly cosmopolitan apostles in his thrall make the millennia fly by. Behind the basilica, a park full of rose beds and mulberry bushes links San Lorenzo with Sant'Eustorgio. (www.sanlorenzomaggiore .com; Corso di Porta Ticinese 39; admission free; ⏱7.30am-12.30pm & 2.30-6.30pm; 🚇Missori)

San Lorenzo Columns
ARCHAEOLOGICAL SITE

2 Map p106, B1

The freestanding row of 16 Corinthian columns from Milan's Mediolanum heyday were salvaged from a crumbling Roman residence and lined up here to form the portico of the new basilica. (Corso di Porta Ticinese; 🚇Missori)

Basilica di Sant'Eustorgio
BASILICA

3 Map p106, B2

Sant'Eustorgio was built in the 4th century to house the supposed bones of the Three Kings, but the real scene-stealer is Pigello Portinari's private chapel. Representative of the Medici bank in Milan, Portinari had the cash to splash on Milan's finest Renaissance chapel, and frescoed it with masterpieces by Vincenzo Foppa. In the centre stands the white marble *Ark of St Peter Martyr*, one of the finest sculpted sarcophagi in Italy. (Piazza Sant'Eustorgio; ⏱7.45am-6.30pm; 🚇2, 3)

Fondazione Prada
EXHIBITION SPACE

4 Map p106, G1

The Fondazione Prada produces two grand-scale solo shows each year in an old warehouse that's impressive enough to give you 'art butterflies' on its own. The likes of Anish Kapoor and Louise Bourgeois, or mid-career mavericks such as Francesco Vezzoli and Nathalie Djurberg, do the space justice. Check website for specific dates. (📞02 5419 2230; www.fondazione prada.org; Via Fogazzaro 36; ⏱11am-8pm Tue-Sun during exhibitions; 🚇3)

Eating

Dongiò
CALABRESE €€

5 Map p106, F2

One of the best value-for-money restaurants in Milan, this big-hearted Calabrese trattoria serves the spicy flavours of the south on delicious homemade pasta. Starters include bountiful platters of southern salami and piquant cheeses. Reservations are recommended. (📞02 551 13 72; Via

Bernardino Corio 3; meals €30-40; ⏱noon-2.30pm & 7.30-11.30pm Mon-Fri, 7.30-11.30pm Sat; 🚼; Ⓜ Porta Romana)

Le Vigne   OSTERIA, MILANESE €€

6 Map p106, A3

Blindfold yourself and point at the menu, because that's the only way to choose among zucchini flowers stuffed with artisanal herbed ricotta, risotto with shrimp and nasturtium flowers, and a salad of octopus, artichoke and zucchini. (📞02 837 56 17; Ripa di Porta Ticinese 61; meals €25-30; ⏱noon-3pm & 7-11pm Mon-Sat; Ⓜ Porta Genova)

Giulio Pane e Ojo   TRATTORIA €

7 Map p106, F2

If all the Roman restaurants in town were this appealing, Milan would probably start calling itself Mediolanum again. Waiters dish up Roman sass when asked to help you choose between the *bucatini amatriciana* (tube pasta with tomato, pecorino cheese and pig's cheek) and *saltimbocca* (veal with sage). At these prices, why not try both? (📞02 545 61 89; www.giuliopaneojo.com; Via Ludovico Muratori 10; meals €15-25; ⏱noon-2pm & 7-10.30pm Mon-Sat; 🚼; Ⓜ Porta Romana)

Basilica di Sant'Eustorgio

Gattullo

PASTICCERIA €

8 Map p106, C2

Gattullo is Milan's finest pasticceria, serving up miniature pastries, tarts, sweets, sandwiches and officially recognised artisan panettone since 1961. Hailing from that great southern baking town Ruvo di Puglia, Joseph Gattullo built his small bakery into an empire bourgeoisie families can't do without. It is still located in its retro '70s premises, with its Murano chandeliers and curved wooden bar. (📞02 5831 0497; www.gattullo.it; Piazzale di Porta Lodovico 2; pastries from €1.50; ☉7am-9pm Sep-Jul; ❄ 📶; 📮3, 9)

Sushi Koboo

JAPANESE €€

9 Map p106, C2

Elegant Sushi Koboo serves delectable sushi, sashimi and tempura at a traditional kaiten (conveyor belt) bar and at tables in several intimate rooms. The atmosphere is warm and welcoming: blond wood, exposed beams and mosaic decorations glow beneath the large, moonlike light fittings. If you're a couple or a group, order the mixed sushi boat, which actually comes in a handcrafted vessel. (📞02 837 26 08; www.sushi-koboo.com; Viale Col di Lana 1; meals €20-35; ☉noon-2.30pm & 7.30-11.30pm Tue-Sun; ❄; 📮3, 9)

Cantina della Vetra

ITALIAN €€

10 Map p106, C1

This country-style place with big windows overlooking the Piazza Vetra sports gingham tablecloths, but otherwise underplays the rustic element. The *salumi* (mixed cured meat) platter includes a mortadella *tartufata*, *lardo* and a pancetta *coppata*, as well as regional salami. It's known for its wine cellar as much as for the hearty regional staples, and books out most nights. (📞02 8940 3843; www.cantinadella vetra.it; Via Pio IV 3; meals €30-40; ☉7.30-11pm Mon-Fri, noon-3pm & 7.30-11pm Sat & Sun; ❄; 📮2, 3, 14)

Sadler

ITALIAN €€€

11 Map p106, B4

Get ready for a serious tummy-filling session and Claudio Sadler's culinary wisdom: Sardinian *fregola* pasta with broad beans, pigeon ragout and cocoa; scabbard fish with borage-and-chickpea fritters; or horse tartare, with crisped parmesan, peppers and fruity black truffles. (📞02 87 67 30; www.sadler.it; Via Ascanio Sforza 77; meals €120; ☉7.30-11pm Mon-Sat; Ⓜ Romolo, 📮3)

Drinking

Cuore

BAR

12 🍷 Map p106, B1

Retro Cuore has heart and soul by the bucket load with its vintage '50s furniture, TVs screening cult films and Hawaiian cocktails including Pina Coladas and Mai Tais. It is popular with students from the nearby Sacro Cuore university and the laid-back *aperitivo* includes a vegan option on request. (📞02 5811 8311; www.cuoremilano.it;

Via Gian Giacomo Mora 3; ⏰6pm-2am;
Ⓜ Missori, 🚃2, 14)

Lacerba
BAR

13 Ⓠ Map p106, E2

A homage to Futurism, Milan's most
infamous art movement, Lacerba
combines a retro bar with a restaurant serving up dishes from Futurist
Marinetti's kooky culinary manifesto
(death to pasta!). To counter all the
violence, speed and surging machin-
ery on the walls, take a hit of the
honey and basil cocktail. There's an
excellent wine selection, too. (📞02 545
54 75; www.lacerba.it; Via Orti 4; ⏰noon-
3pm Mon-Fri, 6.30pm-midnight Mon-Sat;
Ⓜ Crocetta)

Le Trottoir
BAR

14 Ⓠ Map p106, B2

Legendary Le Trottoir is housed in an
ex-customs toll gate on the Darsena
docks and is a good place to move on
to after drinks in Navigli. Drink upstairs in the psychedelic yellow, blue
and red Andrea Pinketts lounge or roll
out onto the pavement with hundreds
of other revellers in summer. (📞02 837
81 66; www.letrottoir.it; Piazza XXIV Maggio 1;
admission €10; ⏰11pm-2am; 🚃3, 9)

Refeel
BAR

15 Ⓠ Map p106, F3

Refeel is part of the stylish Living/
Circle/Exploit family created by Milanese bar maestros Fabio Acampora
and Sebastian Bernandez. As with

their other venues, expect designer
furnishings, lots of blond wood,
concrete and glass, and an enviable
aperitivo buffet featuring focaccia,
tramezzini, grilled vegetables, charcuterie and sashimi. (📞02 5832 4227; www
.refeel.it; Viale Sabotino 20; ⏰7pm-2am Mon-
Sat, noon-4pm Sun; Ⓜ Porta Romana)

Plastic
NIGHTCLUB

16 Ⓠ Map p106, H1

Friday's London Loves takes no
prisoners with an edgy, transgressive
indie mix and Milan's coolest kids.
Dress to impress if you're seeking
entry to art director Nicola Guiducci's
private Match à Paris on Sunday,
which mashes French pop, indie and
avant-garde sounds. (📞02 73 39 96;
www.thisisplastic.com; Viale Umbria 120;
⏰11pm-4am Fri-Sun mid-Sep–Jun; Ⓜ Lodi)

Top Tip

What's On

The tourist office stocks several
entertainment guides in English:
Milano Mese, Hello Milano (www
.hellomilano.it) and *Easy Milano*
(www.easymilano.it).

For club listings, check out
ViviMilano (www.vivimilano.it, in
Italian), which comes out with the
Corriere della Sera newspaper on
Wednesday. *La Repubblica* (www
.repubblica.it, in Italian) is also
good on Thursday. Another source
of inspiration is *Milano-2night*
(http://2night.it/milano).

Magazzini Generali

NIGHTCLUB

17 Map p106, E4

When this former warehouse is full of people working up a sweat to an international indie act, there's no better place to be in Milan. Most gigs are under €20, and there's free entry on other nights when DJs get the party started. (☎02 539 39 48; www.magazzini generali.it; Via Pietrasanta 14; ☺11pm-4am Wed-Sat Oct-May; Ⓜ Lodi, ☒24)

Entertainment

La Salumeria della Musica

CLUB, CULTURAL VENUE

18 ⭐ Map p106, E5

The 'Delicatessen of Music' is a firm favourite with Milan's alternative scene. Come here for new acts, literary salons, cultural events and jazz. Shows start around 10.30pm, and if you get the munchies you can grab a plate of cheese and cold cuts. (☎02 5680 7350; www.lasalumeriadellamusica.com; Via Pasinetti 4; ☺9pm-2am Mon-Sat Sep-Jun; ☒24)

Auditorium di Milano

CLASSICAL MUSIC

19 ⭐ Map p106, B4

Abandoned after WWII, the Cinema Massimo was transformed in 1999 into the state-of-the-art home of Milan's Giuseppe Verdi Symphonic Orchestra and Milan Chorus, as well as a venue for visiting international

San Lorenzo Columns (p108)

jazz acts and chamber music groups. (☎02 8338 9422; www.auditoriumdimilano .org; Largo Gustav Mahler; ☺box office 2.30-7pm Tue-Sun; ☒3, 9)

Scimmie

LIVE MUSIC

20 ⭐ Map p106, B3

Jazz, alternative rock and blues are the stock in trade of the emerging talents who play to overflowing crowds inside, in the garden and on its summertime jazz barge. Concerts start at 10pm. (☎02 8940 2874; www. scimmie.it; Via Cardinale Ascanio Sforza 49; admission €8-15; ☺8pm-3am Mon-Sat; Ⓜ Porta Genova)

Shopping

Biffi   FASHION

21 Map p106, B1

Retailer Rosy Biffi spotted potential in the young Gio and Gianni long before Armani and Versace became household names (more recently, she got Milanese women hooked on US cult-brand jeans). She has a knack for interpreting edgier trends and making them work for conformist Milan; check out her selection of international fashion heavyweights for both men and women. (📞 02 831 16 01; www.biffi .com; Corso Genova 5 & 6; 🕐 3-7.30pm Mon, 9.30am-1.30pm & 3-7.30pm Tue-Sat; 🚊2)

Danese   DESIGN, HOMEWARES

22 🔒 Map p106, D1

Milan's Danese may not be as well known as Piedmont's Alessi, but its products possess the same sense of wit and attention to everyday detail. If Enzo Mari's delightful 'Sea in a Box' puzzle caught your eye at the Triennale di Milano, then this is the place to make one your own. (📞 02 5830 4150; www.danesemilano.com; Piazza San Nazaro in Brolo 15; 🕐2.30-7pm Mon, 10am-1.30pm & 2.30-7pm Tue-Sat; Ⓜ Crocetta)

Etro Outlet   FASHION

23 🔒 Map p106, G1

The ultimate money look – silk ties, cashmere T-shirts, embellished purses and bolts of lavishly patterned fabric – can be had here at plebeian prices. (📞 02 5502 0218; Via Spartaco 3; 🕐3-7pm Mon, 10am-1pm Tue-Sun; 🚊9, 29/30)

Frip   MUSIC

24 🔒 Map p106, B1

A husband-and-wife DJ-stylist duo highlight some of Milan's most avant-garde looks and sounds. Look for Henrik Vibskov print dresses and strap-on gaffer tape jewels or Hixsept shirts; then head straight for the vinyl and CDs. (📞 02 832 13 60; www.frip.it; Corso di Porta Ticinese 16; 🕐3-7.30pm Mon, 11am-2pm & 3-7.30pm Tue-Sat; 🚊3)

Local Life
Zona Tortona

Once a tangle of working-class tenements and factories, Zona Tortona is now flush with design companies, studios and neighbourhood eateries. This is home to the head offices of Diesel and Armani (look for the Tadao Ando–designed Armani Teatro on Via Bergognone). During the Salone del Mobile in April, the area hosts satellite shows, launches and parties – transforming into a destination in itself.

❶ Design Library
Where better to soak up the studied, arty vibe of the zone than a window-side sofa at the **Design Library Cafe** (📞02 8942 3329; www.designlibrary.it; Via Savona 11; ⏰7.30am-10.30pm Mon, 7.30am-11.30pm Tue-Thu, 7.30am-2am Fri, 5pm-2am Sat; ❄; Ⓜ Porta Genova) or get to work at one of the subtly lit tables (white MacBooks match nicely). Near the Porto Genova metro station, the library (yearly

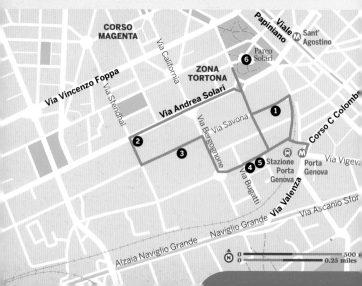

membership €25) is a design buff's dream: it's lined with back issues of *Domus, Abitare* and *Phaidon* design monographs.

❷ Fondazione Arnaldo Pomodoro

Metal-loving Arnaldo Pomodoro's large-scale, sci-fi-tinged work is on show at this vast post-industrial space, but he also launched the **foundation** (📞02 8907 5394; www.fondazionearnaldo pomodoro.it; Via Andrea Solari 35; ⏱11am-6pm Wed-Thu, Sat & Sun, 11am-10pm Fri last entry 1hr before closing; Ⓜ Sant' Agostino) to highlight the work of upcoming sculptors.

❸ Mussels at La Cozz

Moules et frites (mussels and fries) get a Milanese makeover at **La Cozz** (📞02 4771 1145; www.lacozz.it; Via Savona 41; ⏱10am-11.30pm Tue-Sun; Ⓜ Porta Genova). Have them done a number of pan-European ways, from cream and Pernod to rocket and saffron. *Fines de clairs* or Breton oysters come raw or gratined for starters, while desserts like lemon gelati will keep you coming back.

❹ Bigne & Bocci

Drop into old-style **Bigne** (📞02 8728 1464; Via Tortona 21; Ⓜ Porta Genova) and order a quick Campari or a gelati scooped from the retro counter. On a fine Sunday sit outside overlooking the bocci court opposite. Or better yet, play yourself. They have extra equipment available. Big brother **Boccino**

(📞02 8941 5562; www.ristoranteboccino.it; ❇; Ⓜ Porta Genova) next door offers super-stylish dining, especially on the wisteria draped terrace upstairs.

❺ Shop Via Tortona

When Italian *Vogue* art director Flavio Lucchini opened a photographic studio on scruffy Via Tortona in 1983 everyone thought he was mad. But now 'the zone' is a magnet for designers, artists and photographers. Cruise the length of Via Tortona for cult eyewear at **Mafalda 86** (📞333 854 9929; www.mafalda86.it; Via Tortona 19; Ⓜ Porta Genova), jewellery in methacrylate plastic at **iStudio** (📞02 8942 2722; Via Tortona 12; Ⓜ Porta Genova) and funky footwear at **Federea Milano** (📞02 8339 0446; www.federeamilano.it; Via Tortona 12; Ⓜ Porta Genova).

❻ Swimming in Parco Solari

Missoni hosted its first Milan show at the covered **Piscina Solari** (📞02 469 52 78; www.milanosport.it; Via Montevideo 20; €4 Mon-Fri, €5 Sat & Sun; ⏱7am-2.30pm Mon-Fri, 7.30-11pm Tue & Fri, 9.30-11pm Wed, 7am-9am & 1-7pm Sat, 7am-6.30pm Sun; ♿; Ⓜ Sant'Agostino) in 1968, complete with inflatable, floating furniture. It was totally original – no one had seen anything like it – and it persuaded other fashion houses to abandon Florence's Sala Bianca fashion shows in favour of Milan. Today the swimming pool, designed by architect Arrigo Arrighetti and located in leafy Parco Solari, plays a central role in Milan's summer scene.

Explore

Lago Maggiore & Around

More than its neighbours, Lago di Como and Garda, Lago Maggiore has retained the belle époque air of its early tourist heyday, when Napoleon first came to town and ordered the building of the Simplon Pass through the Alps to Switzerland. Attracted by the mild climate and easy access, the European *haute bourgeoisie* flocked to buy and build grand lakeside villas and established a series of extraordinary gardens around its shores.

The Sights in a Day

☀ Toss a coin to determine which palace to start the day with: for romance and intimate family details opt for Palazzo Madre (p118) and for history, art and ostentation try Palazzo Borromeo (p119), where Prince Charles and Princess Diana holidayed in 1985 as guests of the Borromei family.

☀ For lunch make sure you've booked in for fine lakeside dining at **Ristorante Milano** (p123), **Lo Scalo** (p124) or **Taverna del Pittore** (p123), where you should order Lake Maggiore's speciality trout or char and a bottle of wine from nearby Franciacorte vineyards.

☾ After lunch plan on taking it easy with an amble through the tropical hothouses and camellia groves of **Villa Taranto** (p122). Then make the short hop over to Intra for evening *aperitivo* at **La Bottiglieria del Castello** (p125) or movie-star cocktails on the terrace of the **Grand Hotel des Iles Borromées** (p124).

If you're in town on Sunday, or visiting during the month of August, take the fast boat to Cannobio's **lakeside market** (p125) and check out Locarno's **Festival Internazionale di Film** (p123), where you can kick back in front of the open-air screen in Piazza Grande.

👁 Top Sights

Isole Borromeo (p118)

♥ Best of the Lakes

History
Isole Borromeo (p118)

Gardens
Villa Taranto (p122)

Palazzo Madre (p119)

Culture
Villa Giulia (p125)

Festival Internazionale di Film (p123)

Drinking
Grand Hotel des Iles Borromées (p124)

La Bottiglieria del Castello (p125)

Getting There

Ⓜ **Train** Stresa is on the Domodossola–Milan train line and trains leave Milan's Stazione Centrale hourly.

🚢 **Boat** Ferries and hydrofoils on the lake are run by **Navigazione Lago Maggiore** (☎ 800 55 18 01; www.navigazionelaghi.it). There are ticket booths in each town next to the embarkation quay.

Top Sights
Isole Borromeo

The Borromean Gulf forms Lake Maggiore's most beautiful corner, and the Isole Borromeo (Borromean Islands) harbour its most spectacular sights: the privately owned palaces of the Borromei family. Closest to Stresa is Isola Bella with its ostentatious terraces and cool shell-encrusted grottos, while the luxuriant tropical gardens of Isola Madre beckon further afield. Just offshore at Verbania-Pallanza is tiny Isola San Giovanni, once the residence of conductor Toscanini and still the private summer residence of the Borromei family.

◉ Map p120, B5

☑ 0323 3 05 56

www.borromeoturismo.it

combined ticket adult/ reduced €16.50/7.50

◷ 9am-5.30pm Apr-Oct

⛴ Isola Bella, Isola Madre, Isola Superiore

Palazzo Borromeo, Isola Bella

Don't Miss

Palazzo Borromeo

Isola Bella took the name of Carlo III's wife, the *bella* Isabella, in the 17th century, when its centrepiece, **Palazzo Borromeo** (adult/reduced €12.50/5.50), was built. Presiding over 10 tiers of terraced gardens, the baroque palace contains stellar artworks as well as Flemish tapestries and sculptures by Canova. Well-known guests have included Napoleon and Josephine in 1797 (you can see the bed they slept in), and Prince Charles and Princess Di in 1985.

Palazzo Madre

The fabulous **Palazzo Madre** (adult/reduced €10/5.50) *is* the island of Madre. White peacocks with bristling feathers resembling extravagant bridal gowns strut around English-style gardens that easily rival those of Isola Bella, although they retain a more romantic atmosphere. Inside the 16th- to 18th-century palace you'll find the Countess Borromeo's doll collection and a neoclassical puppet theatre care of a La Scala set designer, complete with a cast of devilish marionettes.

Isola Superiore

Tiny 'Fisherman's Island' retains much of its original fishing village atmosphere, and remains a picturesque spot for lunch. Apart from an 11th-century apse and a 16th-century fresco in the Chiesa di San Vittore, there isn't anything to see; so take a seat at one of the portside restaurants and order some grilled lemon perch or char and a glass of Soave.

☑ Top Tips

▶ Give yourself at least half a day to enjoy each palace.

▶ To access the Palazzo Borromeo's fine art collection you need to purchase a separate ticket for the Galleria dei Quadri (€4).

▶ Don't miss the 3000-year-old fossilised boat in the grotto of Palazzo Borromeo.

✕ Take a Break

There's only one cafe on Isola Madre for drinks and snacks. For authentic lake cooking on Isola Bella, go to **Elvezia** (Map p120, B5; ☎0323 3 00 43; meals €30-35; ◷Tue-Sun Mar-Oct, Fri-Sun Nov-Feb). Book ahead out of season.

Isola Superiore has dozens of fish restaurants near the port. **Albergo Verbano** (Map p120, B5; ☎0323 3 04 08; www.hotelverbano.it; Via Ugo Ara 2, Isola Superiore; s €100-120, d €150-185; ◷Mar-Dec) has accommodation and a restaurant overlooking the lake.

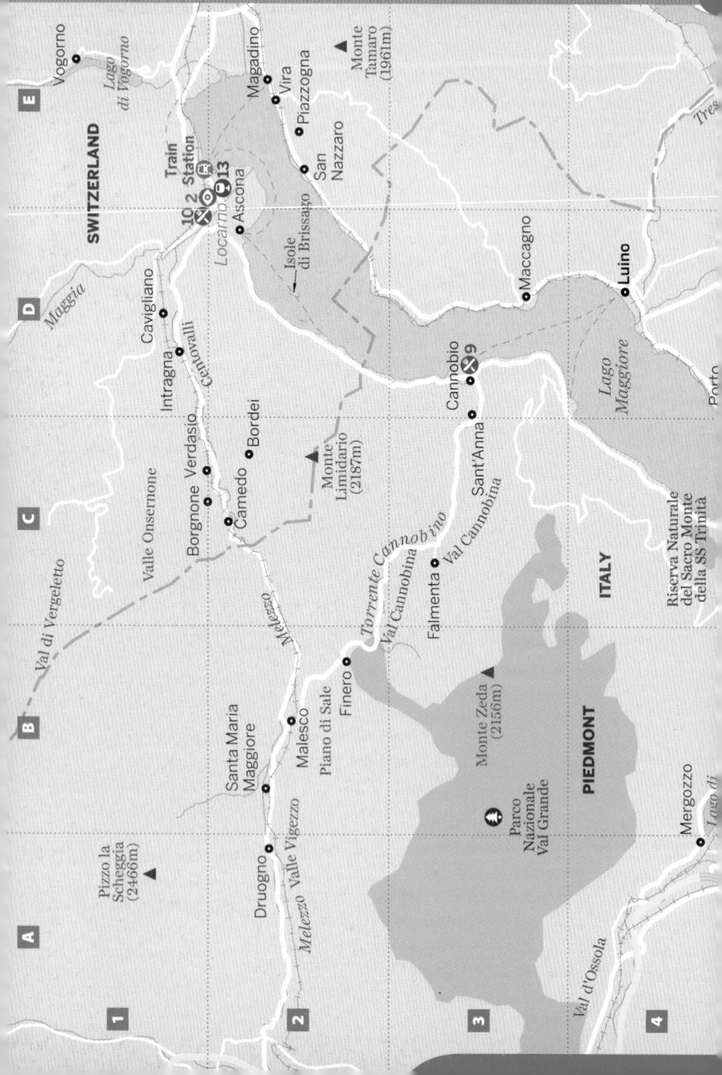

E

Vogorno

Lago
di Vogorno

SWITZERLAND

Maggia

Magadino

Vira

Piazzogna

Monte
Tamaro
(1961m)

Train
Station

13

10 2

Locarno

Ascona

San
Nazzaro

Isole
di Brissago

Maccagno

Luino

Lago
Maggiore

D

Cavigliano

Intragna

Borgnone Verdasio

Centovalli

Camedo

Bordei

Monte
Limidario
(2187m)

Cannobio

9

Sant'Anna

Porto

Tres

Valle Onsernone

Melezzo

Torrente Cannobino

Val Cannobina

Falmenta

Val Cannobina

Riserva Naturale
del Sacro Monte
della SS Trinità

C

Val di Vergeletto

Santa Maria
Maggiore

Malesco

Piano di Sale

Finero

Monte Zeda
(2156m)

ITALY

PIEDMONT

B

Pizzo la
Scheggia
(2466m)

Druogno

Melezzo Valle Vigezzo

Parco
Nazionale
Val Grande

Mergozzo

Lago di

A

Val d'Ossola

1

2

3

4

Cuasso al Monte

LOMBARDY

Parco Regionale Campo dei Fiori
Campo dei Fiori (1226m) ▲

Casalzuigno

⦿ **Varese**

Malnate

Tradate

Castiglione Olona

Schiranna

Capodiago

Voltorre

Gemonio

Gavirate

Bardello

Lago di Biandronno

Bodio

Lago di Varese

Azzate

Riserva Naturale Brabbia

Varano Borghi

Lago di Comabbio

Vergiate

Somma Lombardo

Ticino

For reviews see
⦿ Top Sights   p118
⦿ Sights   p122
⦿ Eating   p123
⦿ Drinking   p124
⦿ Entertainment   p125
⦿ Shopping   p125

5 miles
10 km
N

Sasso del Ferro (1062m) ▲

Intra Verbania

Feriolo Pallanza Verbania

Baveno

Gravellona

Monte Mottarone ▲

Mottarone

Funivia Stresa-Mottarone

Gignese

Omegna ⦿15

Nonio

Oira

Lago d'Orta

Strona

Ronco

Pella

Legro

Orta San Giulio ▲ Sacro Monte

Miasino

Tortirogno

Gozzano

Borgomanero

PIEDMONT

Sacro Monte di San Carlo

Arona ⦿6 ⦿5

Meina

Lesa

Ranco

Angera

Rocca di Angera ●

Sesto Calende

Castelletto del Ticino

Borgo Ticino

Comabbio

Osmate

Lago di Monate

Monate

Ispra

Eremo Santa Caterina del Sasso

Reno ⦿4

Lake Maggiore Express

Laveno ⦿ FNM Train Station

Leggiuno

Lago di Comabbio

Isole Borromeo ⦿1 Villa Taranto ferry

Stresa ⦿ ⦿8 ⦿11 ⦿3

⦿14

Sights

Villa Taranto
BOTANICAL GARDEN

1 Map p120, C5

In 1931, royal archer and Scottish captain Neil McEacharn bought Villa Taranto from the Savoy family and started to plant some 20,000 species over a 30-year period. Near the town of Pallanza, it is considered one of Europe's finest botanical gardens, with rolling hillsides of rhododendrons and camellias, acres of tulips and hothouses full of equatorial lilies. (📞0323 40 45 55; www.villataranto.it; Via Vittorio Veneto 111, Verbania Pallanza; adult/reduced €9.50/5.50; ⏰8.30am-6.30pm; P; 🚢Villa Taranto)

Locarno
SWISS TOWN

2 Map p120, E1

Ruled by Milan's Visconti until 1513, Locarno's latter-day fame comes from pleasure-seeking summer concerts and its international film festival. Wander the old town's cinematic piazzas and lakeside promenade, and admire the fine Lombard art hidden in churches such as the **Chiesa Nuova** (Via Cittadella) and the **Chiesa di San Francesco** (Piazza San Francesco). A rope railway ascends 365m from Locarno to the **Santuario della Madonna del Sasso** (Via del Santuario 2), where Bramantino's *Fuga in Egitto* (Flight into Egypt) captures a soft-faced Mary amid a craggy Lombard landscape. (🚢Locarno)

Statue, Palazzo Borromeo (p119)

Funivia Stresa-Mottarone
CABLE CAR

3 Map p120, B5

Captivating views of the lake unfold during a 20-minute cable-car journey to the top of 1491m-high Monte Mottarone. On a clear day you can see Lago Maggiore, Lago d'Orta and Monte Rosa, on the border with Switzerland. (📞0323 3 02 95; www.stresa-mottarone.it; Piazzale della Funivia, Mottarone; return adult/reduced €17.50/11; ⏰9.30am-5.30pm; 👶; 🚢Stresa) At the midstation (803m), more than 1000 alpine and subalpine species flourish in the **Giardino Botanico Alpini** (📞0323 3 02 95; www.giardinoalpinia.it; adult/reduced €3/2.50; ⏰9.30am-6pm Apr-Oct), a botanical garden dating from 1934.

Eremo di Santa Caterina del Sasso
HERMITAGE

4 Map p120, C5

The hermitage of Santa Caterina del Sasso is one of the most spectacularly located monasteries in northern Italy. Clinging to the high rocky face of Lake Maggiore's southeast shore, about 13km north of Angera, the highlight is the **Church of St Catherine**, which is filled with a carnival of frescoes and consists of three separate sections, connected by a stone pathway. (☏0332 28 61 63; www.santacaterinadelsasso.com; Via Santa Caterina 13, Leggiuno; ☺8.30am-noon & 2.30-5pm Mar-Oct, 9am-noon & 2-5pm Sat & Sun Nov-Feb; ☕Santa Caterina)

Sacro Monte di San Carlo
LANDMARK

5 Map p120, B7

Milan's superstar bishop San Carlo Borromeo (1538–84) was born in Arona. In 1610 he was declared a saint and his cousin, Federico, ordered the creation of a *sacro monte* (sacred mountain), with 15 chapels lining a path uphill to a church dedicated to the saint. The church and three of the chapels were built, along with a hollow, 35m-high bronze-and-copper statue of Charles himself. Commonly known as the colossus, it can be climbed, affording a spectacular view through the giant's eyes. (☏0322 24 96 69; www.piemontesacro .it; Piazza San Carlo, Arona; admission €4; ☺9am-12.30pm & 2.30-6pm Mar-Oct, to 4.30pm Sat & Sun Nov-Feb; 👬; ☕Arona)

Top Tip

Outdoor Film Festival

Locarno has hosted the two-week **Festival Internazionale di Film** (International Film Festival; ☏091 756 21 21; www.pardo.ch; Via Ciseri 23) every August since 1948. Cinemas are used during the day but, at night, films are shown on a giant screen in porticoed Piazza Grande.

Eating

Taverna del Pittore
ITALIAN €€€

6 Map p120, B7

Possibly Lake Maggiore's most romantic restaurant, this Arona taverna has a lakeside terrace and views of the illuminated Rocca di Angera at night. The refined food features *lasagnette* with saffron, fragrant truffle ravioli and a peerless mushroom *tagliata*. (☏0322 24 33 66; www.ristorantetavernadel pittore.it; Piazza del Popolo 39, Arona; meals €60-80; ☺Tue-Sun; ❄; ☕Arona)

Ristorante Milano
CONTEMPORARY ITALIAN €€€

7 Map p120, C5

Antique-filled Ristorante Milano in Verbanias sits off its own garden where a handful of tables are set up and birdsong provides the background music. It overlooks Isolino San Giovanni, where Toscanini once spent his summers, and the menu is strictly local and seasonal featuring fish from the lake, Fassone beef from Piedmont and veggies from the restaurant garden. (☑0323 55 68 15; www.ristorantemilanolagomaggiore.it; Corso Zanitelli 2, Verbania; meals €50-60; ⏱Wed-Sun, lunch Mon Apr-Oct; ❄; ☝Verbania)

Ristorante Il Vicoletto ITALIAN €€

 Map p120, B5

Located a short walk up the hill from the centre of Stresa, Il Vicoletto serves a short, but commendable regional menu including lake trout, wild asparagus and traditional risotto with radicchio and Taleggio cheese. The dining room is modestly elegant with bottle-lined dressers and linen-covered tables, and the local clientele speaks volumes in this tourist town. (☑0323 93 21 02; www.ristoranteilvicoletto. com; Vicolo di Poncivo 3, Stresa; meals €30-45; ⏱lunch & dinner Fri-Wed; ☝Verbania)

Top Tip
Lago Maggiore Express

The **Lago Maggiore Express** (www .lagomaggioreexpress.com; 1 day adult/reduced €26/13, 2 day €33.60/16.80) is a picturesque day trip done under your own steam. It includes train travel from Arona or Stresa to Domodossola, from where you get the charming Centovalli (Hundred Valleys) train to Locarno in Switzerland and a ferry back to Stresa. Tickets are available from Navigazione Lago Maggiore booths at each port.

Lo Scalo CONTEMPORARY ITALIAN €€€

 Map p120, D3

For a romantic dinner, it is hard to beat this lakefront high-flyer in Cambio. The setting is perfect and the cooking is sophisticated and clean, featuring dishes such as ribbon-thin *tagliolini* pasta with cuttlefish, zucchini and roast guinea fowl. (☑0323 7 14 80; www.loscalo.com; Piazza Vittorio Emanuele III 32, Cannobio; meals €60; ⏱Wed-Sun, dinner Tue; ❄; ☝Cannobio)

Osteria Chiara ITALIAN €€

 Map p120, E1

Tucked away on a cobbled lane in Locarno, this has the cosy feel of a *grotto*. Sit at granite tables under the pergola or at timber tables by the fireplace for chunky pasta and mostly meat dishes. From the lake follow the signs up Vicolo dei Nessi. (☑+41 091 743 32 96; www. osteriachiara.ch; Vicolo della Chiara 1, Locarno; mains Sfr16-30; ⏱Tue-Sat; ♿; ☝Cannobio)

Drinking

Grand Hotel des Iles Borromées PIANO BAR

 Map p120, B5

After a stint on the Italian front in 1918, Ernest Hemingway checked himself into Stresa's Grand Hotel, where he wrote the antiwar novel *A Farewell to Arms*. You may not be able to afford a room here – guests have included Princess Margaret and the Vanderbilts – but you can always slug back a Manhattan on the terrace. (☎032 93 89 38; www.borromees.it; Corso Umberto I, 67, Stresa; ☉6pm-late; 🚢Stresa)

La Bottiglieria del Castello

ENOTECA

12 Map p120, C5

Sample mountain cheeses with a glass of Dolcetto in the pretty piazza at Intra Verbania. You'll be upholding a proud tradition, started in 1905 when sister restaurant Osteria Castello served tumblers of wine to millworkers and fishermen who came here to catch up on the daily news. (☎0323 51 65 79; www.osteriacastello.com; Piazza Castello 9, Intra Verbania; ☉Mon-Sat; 🚢Verbania)

Caffé dell'Arte

CAFE-BAR

13 🚢 Map p120, E1

Tucked away in a 14th-century palazzo in the heart of Locarno's Old Town, this stylish *apéro* bar adjoins the Fondazione Patrizio Patelli, a nonprofit gallery featuring the work of local artists. If you're staying overnight, book into the boutique B&B upstairs. (☎+41 091 751 93 33; www.caffedellarte.ch; Via Cittadella 9, Locarno; ☉8.30am-9pm Tue-Sat; 🚢Locarno)

Entertainment

Villa Giulia

CONCERT VENUE

14 ⭐ Map p120, B5

Theatrical Villa Giulia with its towering lemon-yellow facade and

 Top Tip

To Market

Sitting at the foot of a valley, the hamlet of **Cannobio** (Map p120, D3) 15km from the Swiss border, is the prettiest Italian town on the lake.

On Sunday, the town hosts a large market on the waterfront with more than 290 stalls selling speciality meats, wines, cheeses and sweets, as well as nonfood items.

colonnaded balconies provides a scenic backdrop for open-air summer concerts. Originally the home of Bernardino Branca (who invented the famous liqueur, Fernet), it has a cocktail bar overlooking the lake. (☎032 503 249; www.barvillagiulia.it; Corso Zanitello 8, Pallanza Verbania; 🚹; 🚢Verbania)

Shopping

Alessi

OUTLET STORE

15 🔒 Map p120, A5

Established in Omegna in 1921, Alessi went on to transform modern kitchens with ultracool utensils designed by architect-designers, including Achille Castiglioni, Philippe Starck and Zaha Hadid. Go mad in their huge factory outlet, where the whole range is on offer plus special offers and end-of-line deals. (☎0323 86 86 48; www.alessi.com; Via Privata Alessi 6, Omegna; ☉9.30am-6pm Mon-Sat, 2.30-6pm Sun)

PERITIVI
NE BAR

Explore

Lago di Como & Around

Set in the shadow of the snow-covered Rhaetian Alps and hemmed in by steep, wooded hills, Lake Como (also known as Lake Lario) is the most spectacular of the northern Italian lakes. Shaped like an upside-down letter Y, its winding shoreline is scattered with villages, including delightful Bellagio, which sits at the centre of the two southern branches on a small promontory.

The Sights in a Day

☀ For optimal access to all the lake sites, base yourself in Bellagio. Here your morning coffee run will involve a walk through **Villa Melzi's** (p129) elegant lakeside gardens to Piazza Mazzini where you can board the hydrofoil for the gardens of Varenna's **Villa Monastero** (p133), the sculptures in Tremezzo's **Villa Carlotta** (p133) or the shops and sites of Como.

☀ On your way to Como, lunch at **Ittiturismo da Abate** (p134), the only remaining fishing concession on the lake. Be sure to book ahead out of season, as they may be out fishing. In Como take the pleasant lakefront stroll, Passeggiata di Lino Gelpi, past waterfront mansions to arrive on the doorstep of **Villa Olmo** (p132) where you can wander the gardens, enjoy world-class art or laze around the scenic **swimming pool** (p132).

☾ For sunset take a **seaplane** (p132) over the lake or head up to Brunate in the **cable car** (p132) for panoramic views. Then for dinner, reserve a table beside the hearth or on the terrace at **Al Veluu** (p135) and watch the lights on the lake twinkle like stars.

 Top Sights

Bellagio (p128)

 Best of the Lakes

Architecture
Villa Olmo (p132)

Lake Experiences
Aero Club Como (p132)

Lido Villa Olmo (p132)

Villa Monastero (p133)

Fashion
A Picci (p137)

Getting There

Ⓜ **Train** Services from Milan's Stazione Centrale and Porta Garibaldi stations run hourly services to Como San Giovanni station. Trains from Milan's Stazione Nord arrive at Como's lakeside Stazione FNM ('Como Nord Lago' on timetables).

🚢 **Boat** Ferries and hydrofoils on the lake are run by **Navigazione Lago di Como** (☎ 800 55 18 01; www.navigazionelaghi.it). There are ticket booths in each town next to the embarkation quay.

Top Sights
Bellagio

It's impossible not to be charmed by Bellagio's waterfront of bobbing boats, maze of steep stone staircases, dark cypress groves and showy rhododendron-filled gardens. Its peerless position on the promontory jutting out into the centre of the lake made it the object of much squabbling between Milan and Como, hence its ruined fortifications and Como-esque church of San Giovanni, built by Como masters between 1075 and 1125. Although it teems with visitors in summer, if you turn up out of season you'll have the place almost to yourself.

👁 Map p130, D5

📞 031 95 02 04

www.bellagiolakecomo
.com

Piazza della Chiesa 14

Bellagio

Don't Miss

Villa Serbelloni

Bellagio has been a favoured summer resort since Roman times, when Pliny the Younger holidayed on the promontory where **Villa Serbelloni** (☏031 95 15 55; Via Garibaldi 8; adult/reduced €8.50/4.50; ⏰tours 11.30am & 3.30pm Tue-Sun Apr-Oct) now stands. The Romans introduced the olive and laurel trees that dot the vast 20-hectare gardens, which took on their Italianate, English and Mediterranean designs at the beginning of the 19th century. The villa, now privately owned by the Rockefeller Foundation, still hosts scholars and academics, although the gardens, with their unique view of lake's three branches, are open for guided tours.

Villa Melzi

Built in 1808 for Francesco Melzi d'Eril (1753–1816), Napoleon's advisor and VP of the First Italian Republic, neoclassical **Villa Melzi** (www.giardinidivillamelzi.it; Lungo Lario Manzoni; adult/reduced €6/4; ⏰9.30am-6.30pm Mar-Nov) is one of the most elegant villas on the lake. Situated in a peerless position, the lake laps the fringes of its manicured lawns. The neoclassical temple is where Liszt came over all romantic and composed his 1837 sonata dedicated to Dante and Beatrice.

Lake Tours

For a touch of Clooney-esque glamour, consider taking a tour of the lake in one of **Barindelli's** (☏338 211 03 37; www.barindellitaxiboats.it; Piazza Mazzini) slick, mahogany cigarette boats. They offer hour-long sunset tours (€130 for up to 12 people) around Bellagio's headland where you can view the splendour of Villa Serbelloni from the water. They can tailor-make longer itineraries, complete with picnic lunches.

☑ Top Tips

▶ The gardens are at their finest between March and May when the camellias, azaleas, orchids and rhodo-dendrons bloom in profusion.

▶ Book guided tours of the Villa Serbelloni gardens with **PromoBel-lagio** (☏031 95 15 55; www.bellagiolakecomo.com; Piazza della Chiesa 14; ⏰9.30am-1pm Mon, 9.30am-12.30pm & 1.30-4pm Wed-Fri).

▶ Sightseeing from Bellagio is super-easy. Consider the one-day central lake ticket, which gives you unlimited travel to Varenna, Tremezzo and Cadenabbia for €12.

✗ Take a Break

Break for a cappuccino under the arcades of Piazza Mazzini with the patrons of century-old Bar Rossi (p136).

For lunch wander beneath the avenue of lakeside plane trees through the gardens of Villa Melzi d'Eril to Albergo Silvio (p134) for a fine seafood lunch on the terrace.

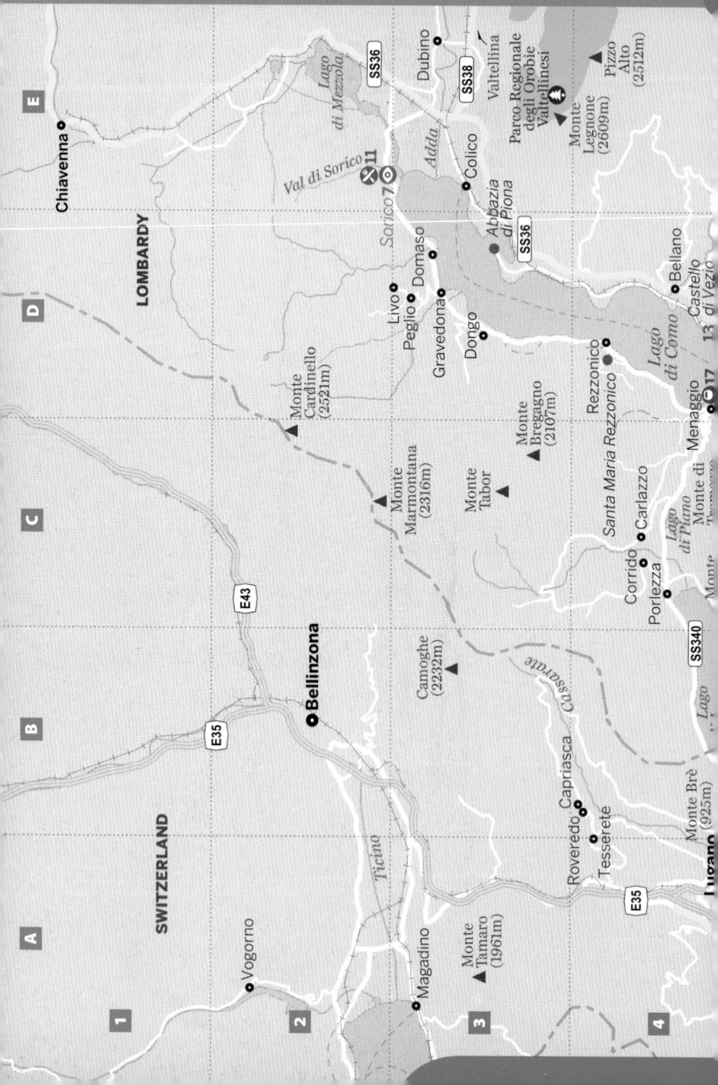

Lago di Mezzola

SS36

Dubino

SS38

Valtellina

Chiavenna

Parco Regionale degli Orobie Valtellinesi

Pizzo Alto (2512m)

Adda

Monte Legnone (2609m)

Colico

Val di Sorico

Sorico

Abbazia di Piona

LOMBARDY

SS36

Livo

Peglio

Domaso

Bellano

Gravedona

Castello di Vezio

Dongo

Lago di Como

Monte Cardinello (2521m)

Rezzonico

Santa Maria Rezzonico

Monte Marmontana (2316m)

Monte Breganno (2107m)

Menaggio

Monte di

Monte Tabor

Carlazzo

Lago di Piano

Corrido

Porlezza

SWITZERLAND

E43

SS340

Camoghe (2232m)

Capriasca

Lago

Bellinzona

E35

Roveredo

Crassarate

Monte Brè (925m)

Tesserete

Ticino

Vogorno

Monte Tamaro (1961m)

Magadino

E35

Lugano

SWITZERLAND

A   B   C   D   E

1   2   3   4

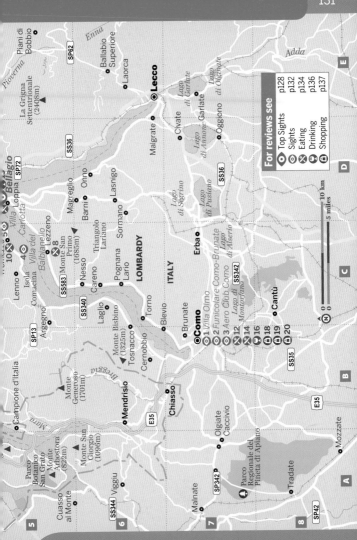

Piani di Bobbio
Enna
Pioverna
La Grigna Settentrionale (2408m)
Ballabio Superiore
Laorca
●Lecco
SP62
Adda
Villa Loppia Bellagio SP72
Villa Carlotta
Lenno
Isola Comacina
Villa del Balbianello
Lezzeno
Mezzegra SP13
Argegno
Nesso
Monte San Primo (1685m)
SS583
Balbianello
Magreglio
Barni
Onno
Lago di Garlate
Lago di Olginate
Civate
Galbiate Garlate
Lago di Annone
Oggiono
Magrate
SS36
Lasngo
SS36
Lombardy
Triangolo Lariano
Sormano
Lago di Segrino
Lago di Pusiano
Erba
Lago di Alserio
Pognana Lario
Careno
Laglio
Monte Bisbino (1325m)
ITALY
Torno
Blevio
Brunate
Funicolare Como-Brunate
●Como
Aero Club Como
Lago di Montorfano
Cantù
Monte Generoso (1701m)
Brezzia
Tosnacco
Cernobbio
Mendrisio
Chiasso
E35
Campione d'Italia
Mura
Monte San Giorgio (1096m)
Viggiù
SS344
Cuasso al Monte
Monte Arbostora (922m)
Parco Botanico San Grato
Olgiate Caccivio
Malnate
Mozzate
Parco Regionale del Pineta di Apiano
Tradate
SP342
E35
SP42

For reviews see

	Top Sights	p128
	Sights	p132
	Eating	p134
	Drinking	p136
	Shopping	p137

5 miles
10 km

1 Villa Olmo
2 Funicolare Como-Brunate
3 Aero Club Como
12 Lago di Montorfano
14 Lago di Alserio
16
18
19
20
SS342
SS35
SS340
SS36

8
10
4

Sights

Villa Olmo
VILLA, MUSEUM

1 ⊙ Map p130, B7

Set grandly facing the lake amid Italianate gardens, the creamy facade of neoclassical Villa Olmo is Como's major landmark. Built in 1728 by the Odescalchi family (relatives of Pope Innocent XI) it now hosts blockbuster art shows in its sumptuous Liberty-style interiors. (☑031 57 61 69; www .grandimostrecomo.it; Via Cantoni 1, Como; adult/reduced €10/8; ⊙9am-8pm Tue-Thu, 9am-10pm Fri-Sun during exhibitions; ∰; ☑Como) During summer the **Lido di Villa Olmo** (Via Cernobbio 2; adult/ reduced full day €6/4, half-day €4.50/2.50; ⊙9am-7pm mid-May–Sep), an open-air swimming pool and lakeside bar, is open to the public.

Funicolare Como-Brunate
CABLE CAR

2 ⊙ Map p130, B7

Northeast along Como's waterfront, past Piazza Matteotti and the train station, is the Como–Brunate cable car, which was built in 1894. It takes seven minutes to reach hilltop **Brunate** (720m), a quiet village offering splendid views. From Brunate scale 143 steps further up to the **Faro Voltiano**. The lighthouseoffers an amazing bird's-eye view of the lake. The Como tourist office can provide a map of walks around Brunate. (☑031 30 36 08; www.funicolare como.it; Piazza de Gasperi 4, Como; one way/

return €2.80/5.10; ⊙8am-midnight mid-Apr–mid-Sep, to 10.30pm mid-Sep–mid-Apr; ∰; ☑Como)

Aero Club Como
SEAPLANE TOURS

3 ⊙ Map p130, B7

For a touch of Hollywood glamour, take one of the 30-minute seaplane tours from Como's Aero Club and buzz Bellagio. Longer excursions over Lake Maggiore and Lake Lugano are also possible. During summer you'll need to reserve at least three or four days in advance. (☑031 57 44 95; www .aeroclubcomo.com; Via Masia 44, Como; flight for 2 people €140; ☑Como)

Villa del Balbianello
VILLA, GARDEN

4 ⊙ Map p130, C5

Located 1km outside Lenno, this was where scenes from *Casino Royale* and *Stars Wars: Attack of the Clones* were shot; it is one of the most dramatic locations on Lake Como. Built by Cardinal Angelo Durini in 1787, it is set amid florid gardens that seem to drip off the high promontory like sauce off a melting ice-cream cone. Visitors are only allowed to walk the 1km path from the Lenno to the estate on Tuesday and at weekends. On other days, you have to take a **taxi boat** (return per person €6). If you want to see the villa, you must join a guided tour (in Italian). (☑0344 5 61 10; www.fondoambiente. it; Via Comoedia 5, Località Balbianello; villa & gardens adult/reduced €12/7, gardens only €6/3; ⊙10am-6pm Tue & Thu-Sun mid-Mar–mid-Nov; ☑Lenno)

Landing stage, Villa del Balbianello

Villa Carlotta

MUSEUM, GARDEN

5 ◎ Map p130, C5

At the 17th-century Villa Carlotta, the botanical gardens are filled with colour in spring from orange trees knitted into pergolas and from some of Europe's finest collections of rhododendrons, azaleas and camellias. The villa, which is strung with paintings, sculptures (especially by Antonio Canova) and tapestries, takes its name from the Prussian princess who was given the place in 1847 as a wedding present from her mother. (☑0344 4 04 05; www.villacarlotta.it; Via Regina 2; adult/reduced €9/5; ☉9am-5pm Easter-Sep, 10am-4pm mid-Mar–Easter & Oct–mid-Nov; ⛴Cadenabbia)

Villa Monastero

VILLA, GARDEN

6 ◎ Map p130, D4

Varenna's former convent of Villa Monastero was transformed into a vast, private residence by the Mornico family between the 17th and 19th centuries. Stroll through the magnificent gardens and enjoy the luxuriant floral, including yucca trees, camellias and magnolias, one of which is said to be 400 years old. The interior is no less extravagant – in the room that fronts the bathroom, the walls are covered in Spanish leather to protect the walls from humidity! (☑0341 29 54 50; villa monastero.eu; Via IV Novembre, Varenna; adult/reduced €5/2; ☉gardens 9am-7pm Mon-Thu, 9am-2pm Fri, house & gardens 2-7pm Fri, 9am-7pm Sat & Sun; ⛴Varenna)

Giro d'Italia

Around Lake Como you'll often espy groups of weekend cyclists kitted out as champions. Just as in any elegant Milan bar, locals like to do things with class. Many follow routes that have been used as stages of the nation's great cycle race, the Giro d'Italia.

Second only to the Tour de France, the Giro has drawn champions from around the world since its inauguration in 1909. A time trial stage in Milan is tradition.

Sorico

FISHING VILLAGE

 7   Map p130, E2

The northernmost towns of Dongo, Gravedona and Sorico once formed the independent republic of the *Tre Pievi* (Three Parishes) and were a hotbed of Cathar heresy. Now they're more popular with watersports enthusiasts than Inquisitors. Sorico, the most northerly of the towns, guards the mouth of the River Mera, which flows into shallow Lake Mezzola, once part of Lake Como and now a bird-breeding nature reserve. Follow the river to the tiny **Oratorio di San Fedelino**, with its 1000-year-old fresco of Christ and the Apostles. It's only accessible on foot or by boat from Sorico. (🚶; 🚢Gravedona, Domaso)

Eating

Ittiturismo Da Abate

LARIAN, SEAFOOD €€

 8   Map p130, C5

Da Abate is located just 8km south of Bellagio in the hamlet of Lezzeno. Run by Claudio and Giuseppe, it is one of the few fish farms left on the lake and is Slow Food recommended. Sample traditional fish specialities such as *lavarello* in balsamic vinegar, linguine with perch and black olives, and the robust-flavoured *missoltino* (fish dried in salt and bay leaves). (📞338 584 38 14; www.ittiturismodabate.it; Frazione Villa 4, Lezzeno; meals €25-35; 🕑dinner Tue-Sun, lunch Sat & Sun; 🚶; 🚢Lezzeno)

Albergo Silvio

CONTEMPORARY LARIAN €€

9   Map p130, D5

Located above the small fishing hamlet of Loppia, a short walk from the centre of Bellagio through the gorgeous Villa Melzi gardens, the terrace restaurant at this family-run hotel (and its views of Villa Carlotta across the lake) is locally renown. The menu focuses largely on lake fish, including lavarello, ravioli stuffed with delicate fish mousse, and Toc, a regional polenta mixed with cheese and cooked over an open fire for two hours. (📞031 95 03 22; www.bellagiosilvio.com; Via Carcano 12, Bellagio; meals €30-50; 🕑Mar–mid-Nov & Christmas week; 🅿 ❄; 🚢Bellagio)

Al Veluu
LARIAN €€€

10 Map p130, C5

Al Veluu is situated on the steep hill-side above Tremezzo with panoramic views from its terrace. Home-cooked dishes are prepared with great pride and reflect the seasonal produce of both the mountains and the lake. Expect butter-soft, milk-fed kid with rosemary at Easter or wild asparagus and polenta. (0344 4 05 10; www .alveluu.com; Via Rogaro 11, Tremezzo; meals €50-70; ⏱Wed-Mon; ⚑; ⛴Cadenabbia)

Agriturismo Giacomino
AGRITURISMO €€

11 Map p130, E2

Situated halfway up the mountain at a height of 1100m and backed by an ancient pine forest, this delightful agriturismo offers awe-inspiring views of Lake Mezzola and delicious, country cooking. Chef Pinuccia serves up a five-course lunch full of farm products, including salami and sausages, rabbit, honey, jams and compotes, and wine from their own cellars. Reservations are essential. (0344 8 47 10; www.agriturismogiacomino.it; Via Fordeccia 42, Bugiallo, Sorico; meals €25-35; P⚑⛴; ⛴Gravedona, Domaso)

Crotto del Sergente
TRATTORIA €€

12 Map p130, B7

This Slow Food–recommended restaurant serving typical Larian (the cuisine of Lago di Como) dishes is set back from the lake in the Como sub-urb of Lora, near the Silk Museum. Sit beneath its atmospheric brick barrel-vaults (a nod to its previous life as a cellar) and dine on artisanal horse salami with chestnuts and honey, or leek *crespelli* (crepes). Be sure to book in advance in summer if you want to sit out on the terrace. (031 28 39 11; www.crottodelsergente.it; Via Crotto del Sergente 13, Como; meals €35; ⏱Thu-Tue, closed Sat lunch; ⛴Como)

Cavallino
TRATTORIA €€

13 Map p130, D4

Sit on Varenna's attractive quayside and enjoy seafood dishes caught by fisherman-proprietor Giordano Valentini. *Primi* (first courses) consist of lake perch and *lavarello* pâté. Also homemade is the *risotto mantecato* (mixed with taleggio cheese to create the 'creamy' effect). With advance booking you can fish with the owner and then eat what you catch. (0341 81 52 19; www.cavallino-varenna.it; Piazza Martiri della Libertà, Varenna; meals €25-35; ⏱Thu-Tue; ⚑; ⛴Varenna)

Trattoria dei Combattenti
TRATTORIA €

14 Map p130, B7

Housed in the building of the Italian Retired Servicemen's association, this popular Como trattoria offers indoor seating at communal tables or outdoor seating in a sunny gravel yard. The cooking is simple and tasty, including grilled meats, salad and chunky seafood pasta. The €14 set

LUCA DA ROS/GRAND TOUR/CORBIS ©

Villa Carlotta (p133)

lunch is good value. (📞 031 27 05 74; Via Balestra 5/9, Como; meals €20; 🕙 Wed-Mon; 🚻; 🚊 Como)

Drinking

Bar Rossi

CAFE-BAR

15 🚇 Map p130, D5

Have at least one coffee in the lovely Art Noveau Bar Rossi, where Bellagio's *bourgeoisie* matrons come to gossip. Set back from the lake, beneath the arcad of Piazza Mazzini, the historical interior is carved Cuban mahogany and was inspired by the Edwardian tearooms that Mr Rossi frequented in the early 20th century. (📞 031 95 01 96; Piazza Mazzini 22-24, Bellagio; snacks €2-6; 🕙 7.30am-midnight Apr-Sep, 7.30am-10.30pm Oct-Mar; 🚊 Bellagio)

Castiglioni

WINE BAR

16 🚇 Map p130, B7

Going strong since 1958, Castiglioni's wonderful deli bar has evolved to include a wine bar and now a restaurant. Sample dozens of local wines with plates of sweet procuitto, or lunch in the pleasant outdoor patio. The menu, which includes all manner of charcuterie plates, lake fish and mountain meat dishes, is surprisingly refined and great value. (📞 031 26 33 88;

www.castiglionistore.com; Via Cesare Cantù 9, Como; ⏲Mon-Sat, lunch noon-2.30pm; 🚢Bellagio, Cadenabbia)

Il Gabbiano
BAR

17 Map p130, D4

About 3km north of Cadenabbia, Menaggio has a cute cobblestone centre, and a square overlooking the lake. Arranged along the waterfront are a couple of cafes that are perfect for lake-gazing and people-watching. Il Gabbiano has the best terrace. Order an ice cream or a glass of wine and sit back and enjoy the laid-back vibe. (📞0344 3 26 08; http://barilgabbiano .com; Lungolago Castelli 25, Menaggio; ♿; 🚢Menaggio)

Shopping

A Picci
SILK SHOP

18 Map p130, B7

Open since 1919, this is the last remaining silk shop in town dedicated to selling Como-designed-and-made silk products such as ties, scarves, throws and sarongs. Products are grouped in price category (starting at €15 for a tie) reflecting the skill and workmanship involved in each piece. (📞031 26 13 69; Via Vittorio Emanuele II 54, Como; ⏲3-7.30pm Mon, 9am-12.30pm & 3-7.30pm Tue-Sat; 🚢Como)

La Tessitura
OUTLET STORE

19 Map p130, B7

Mantero, one of the biggest names in Como silk, runs this large-scale outlet-style store on the site of their former factory (which has now moved out of town). If you can print and weave it, you'll find it here. (📞031 32 16 66; http:// conceptstore.latessitura.com; Viale Roosevelt 2A, Como; ⏲11am-9pm Tue-Sat; 🚢Como)

Enoteca da Gigi
WINE SHOP

20 Map p130, B7

Wines, vintage whiskies and grappas, along with olive oils and balsamic vinegars, line the walls of this sociable Como wine shop and bar.. Drop by in the evening for a glass of Prosecco or a Sauvignon Blanc (from around €2) and enjoy the free, freshly prepared bruschetta. (📞031 26 31 86; www.enoteca gigi.com; Via Luini 48, Como; ⏲9am-1pm & 2.30-8pm Mon-Fri, 9am-9pm Sat, 11am-9pm Sun; 🚢Como)

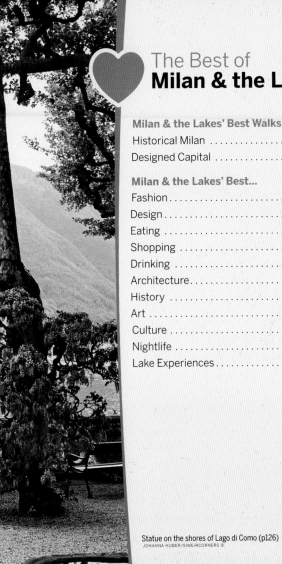

The Best of
Milan & the Lakes

Statue on the shores of Lago di Como (p126)
JOHANNA HUBER/SIME/4CORNERS ©

Best Walks
Historical Milan

🏃 The Walk

From the Caesars to Mussolini, Milan's strategic position has made for a fascinating history. Mercantile Milan invented the idea of the city-state and the Edict of Milan (AD 313) ended the persecution of Christians. From Roman origins to Republican ambitions and industrial pretensions, this walk takes you through Milan's most tumultuous events.

Start Piazza di Duomo; metro Duomo

Finish Piazza Sempione; metro Moscova

Length 3.2km; 1½ hours

🍴 Take a Break

Liberty-style Bar Magenta (p99) on Corso Magenta is a good mid-point stop for a coffee or snack. Otherwise, plan to finish with a picnic in Parco Sempione or *aperitivo* at Bar Bianco (p81).

Castello Sforzesco (p76)

❶ The Duomo

Milan's pearly-white **Duomo** (p26), covered in a pantheon of marble saints, is the third-largest in the world. A gift from Gian Galeazzo Visconti, who started works in 1386, its centuries-long creation maps much of the history of Milan.

❷ Biblioteca Ambrosiana

Blazing an intellectual trail out of the Middle Ages, Cardinal Federico Borromeo founded one of Italy's greatest libraries, the **Biblioteca Ambrosiana** (p34), in 1609. Among its collection are pages from da Vinci's compendium of drawings, the *Codex Atlanticus*.

❸ San Lorenzo Columns

Roman Mediolanum once had its forum in Piazza Carrobbio. Nearby, the 16 Corinthian columns that now stand as portico to the **Basilica di San Lorenzo** (p108) were originally part of a Roman temple or bath. On Via Edmondo de Amicis are the remains of the amphitheatre.

❹ Basilica di Sant'Ambrogio

Sant'Ambrogio (p97) was built on a paleo-Christian burial site and houses the bones of Milan's favourite bishop, Saint Ambrose. Its mongrel Lombard–Romanesque style speaks volumes of history. The oldest part is the apse, with 4th-century mosaics depicting the *Miracle of St Ambrose*.

❺ Tempio della Vittoria

Around the corner from the Basilica, the **Temple of Victory** commemorates 10,000 victims of the 'Great War'. Designed by Giovanni Munzio, its unadorned appearance caused controversy in depressed, postwar Milan where Mussolini was gaining support for his newly formed Blackshirts.

❻ Museo Archeologico

Foundation walls of Roman Milan and a medieval tower form part of Milan's **Archaeological Museum** (p98), which has a model of the Roman city and remnants of glass, grave goods and jewellery in its galleries. Next door Bernardino Luini covered the walls of San Maurizio with frescoed saints.

❼ Castello Sforzesco

Sforza fortress and Milan landmark, this turreted **castle** (p76) embodies Milan's chameleon-like survival instincts. The art within it charts the rise and fall of the city's fortunes and from its ramparts you can look out over Parco Sempione to Napoleon's Arco della Pace.

Best Walks
Designed Capital

🏃 The Walk

Milan's grab bag of architectural styles marks the city's restless evolution into a modern metropolis. From neoclassical shopping malls and Baroque palazzi to 19th-century boulevards lined with Liberty-style apartments and Rationalist villas, take a stroll through the centuries on this walk.

Start Piazza di Duomo; Ⓜ Duomo

Finish Piazza Duca d'Aosta; Ⓜ Centrale FS

Length 4.5 km; two hours

✕ Take a Break

Stop in the Quad for a stylish *cappuccino* and mini *cornetto* (croissant) at Cova (p48). For lunch and evening *aperitivo*, press on to the HClub (p53)

JEAN-PIERRE LEXCOURRET/GETTY IMAGES ©

Casa degli Omenoni

❶ The Gallery

The glass-and-steel **Galleria Vittorio Emanuele II** (p34) is the direct progenitor of the modern shopping mall. It is home to some of the oldest shops and cafes in Milan, including historical **Biffi** (p99), founded in 1867 by royal pastry chef Paolo Biffi, and **Savini**, where Charlie Chaplin declared, 'I've never eaten so well.'

❷ The House of Telamons

Wander north to Via degli Omenoni to enjoy the marvellous giants holding up the balcony of the **Casa degli Omenoni** (House of the Telamons), a 16th-century artist's residence. The vigorous Michelangelesque giants with their bulging muscles and bent backs became a reference for Milanese decorative architecture.

❸ The Golden Quad

Lined with global marques, Via Montenapoleone is the heart of the **Fashion District**. It follows the line of the old Roman wall and was once lined with small grocers and haberdashers, which served the stately mansions. Look out for Palazzo Melzi di Cusano, Palazzo Gavazzi and the **Museo Bagatti Valsecchi** (p51) with their fabulous Renaissance home decor.

4 Villa Necchi-Campiglio

After the Great War, Milan's architects embraced the brave new world of modernism, none more so than Piero Portaluppi, whose signature style of Art Deco and Rationalist rigour is stamped all over town. A highlight is the **Villa Necchi Campiglio** (p35) with its terrarium, radical electronic shutters and Milan's first domestic swimming pool.

5 Casa Galimberti

Tracing the eastern boundary of the Giardini Pubblici, Europe's first public park, Corso Venezia is lined with neoclassical and Liberty-style palaces. The area reached its fashionable zenith in the 1920s when Art Noveau was all the rage. On Via Malpighi the **Galimberti house** (No 3) typifies the style with its exuberant ceramic facade and twirling wrought-iron balconies.

6 Pirelloni

End at the Mesopotamian-style **Stazione Centrale** (1925–31; p82). Adorned with winged horses, medallions and mosaic panelling, it is the largest train station in Italy. In answer to its fanciful Art Deco formula, Giò Ponti's sleek **Torre Pirelli** (1955–60; p82) stands opposite, shooting skywards with a graceful, modern lightness.

Best
Fashion

Milan began to turn heads after WWII when Italy's fashion industry out grew the workshops of Florence. Today the roll call of designers in the Quadrilatero d'Oro make for a glamorous jaunt for any fashion-addict. Paris, New York and London may have equally influential designers, but they can't compete with an industry town that lives and breathes fashion and takes retail as seriously as it does biotech or engineering.

Big Brand Allergy

Younger labels and multibrand retailers can be found in Brera, Corso Como and Corso Vercelli, while giant Rinascente offers diffusion labels for men, women and children. For the Milanese version of high-street shopping, try Porta Ticinese, Via Torino and Corso Buenos Aires, but for Milan's most alternative and avant-garde shopping head to Navigli and the Zona Tortona.

Best Only in Milan

G Lorenzi Specialists in the finest quality men's grooming products. (p49)

Frip DJ-stylist duo highlight some of Milan's most avant-garde looks. (p113)

La Vetrina di Beryl Known to shoe cultists around the world, Barbara Beryl's only shop is in Milan. (p70)

Best Stylist's Eye

10 Corso Como The world's most hyped concept store stuffed with desirable things. (p89)

Aspesi The alma mater of classic Milanese style. (p55)

Casadei It-girl shoes in lollipop hues from Quinto and Flora Casadei. (p56)

A Picci The last silk shop in Como, selling the world's finest quality silks. (p137)

Best Designer Outlets

Il Salvagente Tightly packed racks with discounted Prada, Armani and Versace. (p40)

Etro Outlet The ultimate money look at affordable prices. (p113)

10 Corso Como Outlet Genuine bargains on big-brand names. (p89)

Best Vintage

Superfly Disco diva heaven, Superfly stocks '60s and '70s hot pants and minidresses. (p105)

Cavalli e Nastri Carefully curated early- to mid-20th-century Italian fashion label. (p69)

Vintage Delirium Franco Jacassi's multilevel store stocks a pristine vintage collection. (p89)

Best **Design**

Milan today is home to all the major design showrooms and the site of an endless round of influential international design fairs, and continues to be a centre of design education and publishing. Design here isn't merely functional (although the modernist ideal of creating useful objects is always at its core); it is also suffused with emotion: expressive, inventive, humorous and individual.

PAOLO CORDELLI/GETTY IMAGES ©

Who's Who

A visit to the Design Museum at the Triennale (p78) is a wonderful way to pay homage to the work of Italy's best and brightest. May of these called, or continue to call, Milan home. The names to watch out for include Giò Ponti, Bruno Munari, Piero Fornasetti, Enzo Mari, the Castiglioni brothers, Gaetano Pesce, Mario Bellini, Gae Aulenti, Ettore Sottsass and Alessandro Mendini.

Best Design Inspiration

Triennale di Milano Museum, educational facility and showroom, the Triennale has championed design since the 1930s. (p78)

Studio Museo Achille Castiglioni Tour the studio of one of Italy's most influential 20th-century designers. (p82)

Museo Nazionale della Scienza e della Tecnologia Contains a vast and intriguing collection, including models of da Vinci's machines. (p94)

Design Library Flick through pages of classic designs in back issues of *Domus*, *Abitare* and *Ottogono*. (p114)

Fiera Milano Venue of the Furniture Fair, Fuksas' glass-and-steel sail is an architectural wonder in itself. (p84)

Best Showrooms

È de Padova Six floors of great modern designs curated by guru Maddalena de Padova. (p41)

Spazio Rossana Orlandi An iconic interior's 'space' with out-of-the-ordinary objects and homewares. (p101)

Alessi All your favourite Alessi homewares are now housed in a fabulous new flagship store designed by Martí Guixé. (p49)

Best Eating

Milan's dining scene is much like its fashion scene, with new restaurant openings hotly debated and seats at Michelin-starred tables hard to come by. Whether it's dyed-in-the wool traditional or contemporary fusion cuisine, you'll eat some of Italy's most memorable and sophisticated food here.

The Milanese Larder

The food of Milan may not be redolent of the sun, like that of the south, but its quintessential dishes are still richly golden-hued. *Cotoletta,* sliced buttery veal with a burnished breadcrumb crust, and mellow yellow risotto Milanese (Po Valley *carnaroli* rice enriched with bone marrow and tinted with saffron) are cases in point. Other gold standards include *osso bucco,* a veal shank stew scattered with *gremolata* (parsley, garlic and lemon rind); the polenta that accompanies meat or mushroom dishes; pumpkin-stuffed sage-scented ravioli; *panettone,* the eggy, brioche-like Christmas bread; *mostarda di frutta,* Cremona's mustard-laced sweet preserves, and Lombardy's rich bounty of cheese.

Further Afield

Genovese and Piedmontese dishes often share the menu: *trofie* (pasta twists) with pesto, potatoes and green beans and onion-strewn focaccia here; *bollito misto* (mixed boiledmeats) and *fonduta* (fondue) there. As well as the food of these near neighbours, Milan's generations of immigrants mean that dishes from Lazio, Campania, Tuscany and Puglia are easy to find. The city's increasingly diverse global population is also reflected in the its eating habits. Japanese and Chinese restaurants are commonplace and the cuisines of India, the Middle East and Africa are all represented.

☑ Top Tips

▶ All high-end and popular restaurants should be booked ahead for Friday and Saturday dinner and Sunday lunch. Book *all* meals during Furniture Fair and Fashion Week.

Best Modern Italian

Sadler Culinary verve via Michelin-starred dining on the Naviglio Grande canal. (p110)

Trussardi alla Scala Andrea Berton runs this sexy place overlooking La Scala. (p36)

Pescheria da Claudio *Carpaccio* (sliced raw beef), tuna *tartare* and *frutti di mare* with a contemporary twist. (p67)

Gelati at Grom (p37)

Il Teatro The signature restaurant of the Four Seasons Hotel. (p52)

Best Classics

Ristorante Solferino Has served *osso buco*, *cotoletta* (veal cutlets) and risotto since 1909. (p66)

Da Giacomo Thirty years of faultless service and quality Tuscan cuisine have earned Da Giacomo a loyal following. (p36)

Latteria di San Marco A family concern with Arturo in the kitchen and his wife and daughters waiting tables. (p66)

Maxelâ This regional franchise brings the tradition of Tuscan *bistecca Fiorentina* to Milan. (p66)

Trattoria da Pino A working man's place that's still true to its roots. (p36)

Best International

Sushi Koboo Top quality sushi at surprisingly reasonable prices makes Sushi Koboo outrageously popular. (p110)

Lon Fon No red lanterns and no bric-a-brac, just home-cooked Cantonese with a few seasonal twists. (p52)

Lyr Contemporary Lebanese food amid luxurious baroque furnishings. (p84)

Best Pasticcerie

Gattullo Retro '70s premises and fully certified, artisanal panettone. (p110)

Princi Trays of artisanal breads, pastries and desserts amid beautiful modern decor. (p67)

Biffi Pasticceria Impeccably dressed waiters, flawless service and a polished wooden counter stuffed with wicked treats. (p99)

Best Gelati

Grom Organic, seasonal ice creams, sorbets and granita with Battifollo biscotti. (p37)

Gelateria Marghera Milan's most famous gelateria serving ice-cream cake alongside the classics. (p99)

Shockolat Playing flavour favourite with milk, dark, white, chilli, *gianduja* and cinnamon chocolate. (p99)

Best
Shopping

Aside from fashion and design, Milan's shopping scene is diverse and vibrant, spanning the spectrum from artisanal ateliers to concept shops and lifestyle stores. Guilds as diverse as jewellers, bakers, carpenters and milliners (who derived their name from the city in the 16th century) have catered to the European aristocracy for centuries, so quality and choice are appropriately superb.

Best Food & Wine

Peck Historical Peck is crammed with speciality meats, cheeses, pastries, oils, pastas, chocolates and wine. (p40)

N'Ombra de Vin More than 3000 different labels in the vaulted cellars of a former Augustinian refectory. (p68)

Rinascente The 7th-floor food heaven of Rinascente incorporates a mozzarella bar and an indoor-outdoor restaurant. (p41)

Best Independent Designers

Monica Castiglioni Self-taught jeweller and daughter of design great Achille Castiglioni. (p89)

Calé Fragranza d'Autore A family run perfumier offering artisanal fragances. (p100)

Borsalino This historical hat manufacturer Borsalino has even been showcased at the Triennale. (p38)

Best Souvenir Shopping

Art Book Triennale Beautifully produced art monographs and children's books. (p79)

Fabriano Resource your desk with the most fashionable accessories and notebooks. (p70)

Habits Culti Minimalist homewares and gorgeously packaged room fragrances. (p57)

Citta del Sole Hand-crafted toys, tactical and strategic games, building kits and boomerangs. (p41)

☑ **Top Tips**

▶ Shopping hours are 3pm to 7pm Monday, and 10am to 7pm Tuesday to Saturday, though smaller shops may take a break from 12.30pm to 3pm.

▶ Non-EU citizens can claim back the value-added tax on purchases more than €154.94 at shops displaying a 'Tax Free Shopping' sign. Rinascente has a tax-free centre; otherwise claim your refund at the airport.

Best
Drinking

Like everything in Milan, drinking is a stylish affair and an opportunity to make *la bella figura* (a good impression). *Aperitivo*, or happy hour, stretches from 6pm to 9pm, though the Milanese rarely get there before 7pm. Expect your cocktails to be expertly mixed and joined by a tasty, complimentary and sometimes fabulous buffet. Finally, getting drunk or otherwise messy is *molto vulgare*.

SPAZIO FOTO MEREGHETTI/ALAMY ©

Best Big Night Out Aperitivo

Bulgari Expect vintage liquors, expertly mixed cocktails and high-brow aperitivo. (p67)

HClub The buffet at the Sheraton's bar is legendary and the low-lit garden romantic. (p142)

Grand Hotel des Iles Borromées Drink a Manhattan on the terrace overlooking Lago Maggiore, just as Hemingway did. (p124)

10 Corso Como Concept cocktails beneath a canopy of fairy lights make this Milan's best lifestyle bar. (p89)

Best Wine Cellars

N'Ombra de Vin Tastings can be had all day at the vaulted cellars. (p68)

La Bottiglieria del Castello Sip the finest regional wines in Intra's pretty cobbled piazza. (p125)

Caffeteria degli Atellani Sample unusual Italian vintages in Atellani's glowing glasshouse. (p68)

Best Party Scene

Pandenus A former bakery with an a burgeoning buffet and well-priced drinks. (p53)

Le Trottoir Psychedelic decor and live music in a former dock house on the Darsena. (p111)

Bar Bianco Right in the heart of Parco Sempione, this is *the* place to drink in summer. (p140)

☑ **Top Tips**

▶ During happy hour drinks prices range from €4 to €8, but be prepared to fork out up to €15 at more luxe establishments. Usually the higher the drink price, the more lavish the buffet. At €8-plus, you can expect to see platters of charcuterie and cheeses, *pizzetta*, salads and even pasta.

Best
Architecture

Milan's architectural charm lies in its mix of styles, and at the fore is Italy's 20th-century design heritage. Wide streets are lined with elegant fin-de-siècle Liberty apartments that merge with 1930s Rationalist rigour, while out of the postwar devastation two of the world's unique skyscrapers arose in the form of BBPR's Torre Velasca and Giò Ponti's Torre Pirelli.

Expo 2015

The Milanese often carp that despite claims they are Italy's most modern city, they've not been able to produce a significant building for more than 50 years. This is about to change: the sound of jack-hammers around Stazione Garibaldi signifies the emergence of the Porta Nuova development, with César Pelli's shard-like skyscraper, apartments with hanging gardens and a sunken piazza, while the 420-acre Expo site in Rho and Pero promises a futuristic new skyline from international archi-stars Zaha Hadid, Arata Isozaki, Pier Paolo Maggiora and Daniel Libeskind (www.expo2015.org).

Best Exteriors

Duomo Cloud-piercing Gothic spires in cloudy Candoglian marble. (p26)

Villa Olmo Neoclassical Olmo, with its impressive colonnaded facade, was remodelled in the 'modern fashion'. (p132)

Stazione Centrale Deco-tinged, neo-Babylonian architecture epitomising the nationalist fervour of Fascism. (p82)

Torre Pirelli The tapered sides of Ponti's modernist icon shoot skywards with dynamic modernity. (p82)

Best Interior Decor

Villa Necchi Campiglio Restored 1930s villa designed by Rationalist architect Piero Portaluppi. (p35)

Chiesa di Santa Maria Presso di San Satiro Bramante's trompe-l'oeil apse plays cleverly with perspective. (p34)

Fiera Milano An awesome undulating, steel-and-glass canopy that appears to billow weightlessly like a sail in the breeze (p84)

Portinari Chapel Milan's finest Renaissance chapel with masterly frescoes by Vincenzo Foppa. (p108)

Casa Museo Boschi-di Stefano An Art Deco apartment with postwar furnishings and artworks by De Chirico. (p50)

Best
History

GLYN THOMAS/ALAMY ©

The Romans didn't consider wild Cisalpine Gaul part of Italy at all. In 222 BC when they conquered the city of the Insubri Celts they named it Mediolanum (middle of the plains). Since then Milan has been home to Imperial courts, supplied arms for various empires and flourished on the back of clever politicking, manufacturing and well-managed farming.

Best Roman Remains

Civico Museo Archeologico Home to Roman, Greek and Etruscan artefacts and a model of Roman Milan. (p98)

San Lorenzo Columns Has 16 freestanding columns salvaged from a Roman residence and is now an *aperitivo* hotspot. (p108)

Best Medieval Milan

Castello Sforzesco Home of the Visconti and Sforza dynasties who ruled Renaissance Milan, and now the reposi-

tory of splendid period artworks. (p76)

Biblioteca Ambrosiana Houses Leonardo da Vinci's priceless sketchbook, the *Codex Atlanticus*. (p34)

Isole Borromeo The island palaces of the Borromei of Milan, who possess fishing rights over Lake Maggiore, as they have since the 1500s. (p118)

Basilica di Sant'Ambrogio With its medieval masterpieces, magnificent gold altar and sky of gold, this is the resting place of Saint Ambrogio. (p97)

Best Modern Milan

Duomo Napoleon chose Milan as capital of his Cisalpine Empire and finally finished the Duomo, where he was crowned. (p26)

Palazzo Reale Destroyed by WWII bombs, this Visconti palace is now a museum, preserving one damaged hall as a grim reminder. (p34)

Cimitero Monumentale The final resting place of Milan's good burghers, including an epic memorial to those who died in WWII. (p82)

Best
Art

Milan's museums contain collections from the early Renaissance to the neoclassical. What's more, you can often linger with a Bellini or Caravaggio without the usual crowds, even in Milan's most famous gallery, the Brera Pinacoteca. The city is also a treasure trove of 20th-century art. At the Museo del Novecento, the work of Futurists Umberto Boccioni and Giacomo Balla is, a hundred years on, still shockingly fresh.

Painter at Court

Leonardo da Vinci (1452–1519) arrived in Milan from the Medici court in 1482, seeking the patronage of Ludovico Sforza, who was attempting to remake Milan as the perfect city. From his *Portrait of a Young Man* (c 1486) and portraits of Ludovico's mistresses, *The Lady with the Ermine* (c 1489) and *La Belle Ferronière* (c 1490), Leonardo transformed the rigid conventions of portraiture to depict individual images imbued with effortless naturalism. Then he evolved concepts of idealised proportions and the depiction of internal emotional states (*St Jerome*; c 1488), which cohered in his masterpiece *Il Cenacolo*, which expresses the reactions of the Apostles to Christ's announcement that one will betray him.

Modern Italians

With the opening of the Museo del Novecento in 2010, Milan finally got the 20th-century art museum it deserved. Its galleries showcase an extraordinary collection of Italian painting, including the 19th-century Divisionists, the dynamism of Futurism and the 1960s Arte Povera movement. Other noteworthy collections can be found in Villa Necchi Campiglio, the Jesi Collection at the Pinacoteca di Brera and the Casa Museo Boschi-di Stefano.

Best Frescoes

Il Cenacolo Not strictly a fresco at all, Leonardo da Vinci's *Last Supper* breaks all the rules. (p93)

Chiesa di San Maurizio Seventy years in the making, San Maurizio's floor-to-ceiling frescoes still dazzle onlookers. (p97)

Portinari Chapel Vincenzo Foppa was a pioneering figure in the Renaissance in Lombardy, and these are his finest works. (p108)

Best Period Collections

Musei d'Arte Antica The Castle's stellar collection of Ancient Art includes Michelangelo's moving *Rondanini Pietà*. (p76)

Annunciation by Vincenzo Foppa (1468)

Pinacoteca di Brera
A staggering roll call of masters from Titian and Tintoretto to Caravaggio and Bellini. (p60)

Museo Poldi-Pezzoli
Renaissance treasures displayed in equally artful historically styled rooms. (p46)

Museo Bagatti Valsecchi
The Bagatti Valsecchi palazzo is a living museum to the Quattrocento. (p51)

Best 20th-Century Greats

Museo del Novecento
Has 4000 sq metres designed by Italo Rota to showcase Italy's 20th-century talent. (p32)

Villa Necchi Campiglio
Home of Pavian heiresses, Nedda and Gigina, who had a canny eye for big-ticket artworks. (p35)

Casa Museo Boschi-di Stefano
20th-century greats crowded salon-style in a Piero Portaluppi-designed apartment. (p50)

Best Private Foundations

Fondazione Trussardi
Trussardi's nonprofit arm creates and promotes contemporary shows in unusual public venues (p69).

Fondazione Prada
Prada's cultural foundation curates two blockbuster contemporary art shows each year. (p69)

Worth a Trip

Northeast of the centre is **Hangar Bicocca** (☎ 02 853 531 764; www.hangarbicocca.it; Via Chiese 2; ⏱ 11am-7pm Tue, Wed & Fri-Sun, 2.30-10pm Thu; Ⓜ Sesto Marelli) in a former Pirelli industrial site. Its temporary shows are worth a look, but the big attraction is a permanent installation by Anselm Kiefer. The seven concrete-and-lead towers of *The Seven Heavenly Palaces* are a teetering 15m tall and invoke the the abject destruction of postwar Europe.

Best
Culture

The city of Verdi and Puccini has been home to some of the world's foremost classical musicians for at least two centuries. Home to Italy's major music publishers, Milan is also on the international tour circuit of the best European and North American music acts, theatre and dance troupes and, in summer, the city hosts a wicked line-up of cultural festivals.

Best Classical Music

La Scala Frock-up for a night of ballet or opera at Italy's most famous opera house. (p30)

Auditorium di Milano Home of the legendary Giuseppe Verdi Orchestra. (p112)

Blue Note The largest and most prestigious of Milan's jazz venues. (p87)

Villa Giulia A program of summer concerts on the shore of Lake Maggiore. (p125)

Best Festivals

Duomo Lent comes late to Milan with Carnival held on Saturday (after every-

one else's Fat Tuesday) in Piazza di Duomo. (p26)

Navigli Music, food, parades and special events are held along the canals in Navigli's June festival. (p104)

Locarno Film Festival After Cannes and Venice, Locarno has the prettiest venue for screenings: outdoors in Piazza Grande. (p123)

Basilica di Sant'Ambrogio The feast day of Milan's patron saint is celebrated on 7 December with a huge Christmas fair. (p97)

Best Sporting Events

Giro d'Italia Cheer on the pink jersey at the finish

line as this world-famous cycling race winds up in Milan in June. (p134)

San Siro Inter and AC Milan fans flock to San Siro Stadium for Serie A in September. (p98)

Castello Sforzesco In November, join 5000 runners on the Milan City Marathon that starts and finishes at the castle. (p76)

Best Theatre

Piccolo Teatro A risk-taking repertory with a program of ballet and *commedia dell'arte*. (p38)

Piccolo Teatro Strehler Generally acknowledged as the city's top theatre venue. (p69)

Best
Nightlife

Milan's nightlife traverses the spectrum from blandly commercial to cutting edge, but glamming-up applies across the board. Entry runs from €10 to upwards of €20. While club popularity is surprisingly stable – Plastic has been in the business for 24 years – keeping up with nights and DJs is not easy. *Zero*'s fortnightly guide is useful, as is Milano2night (www.milano tonight.it).

GIOVANNI TAGINI/ALAMY ©

Best For Glamour

Il Gattopardo Crystal chandeliers and cream chaise longue in a deconsecrated 19th-century church. (p86)

Armani Privé Dress to impress, Armani's clientele are as beautfiul as the surroundings. (p55)

Best Big Nights Out

Plastic According to Andy Warhol, the sexiest and most transgressive club in town. (p111)

Magazzini Generali Caters to all tastes with a mixture of house, techno, electro and chart classics. (p112)

Nuova Idea Milan's premier gay venue with two dance floors, one for ballroom dancing! (p87)

Alcatraz Founded by Italian rockstar Vasco Rossi, this 1800 sq metre garage rocks a huge weekend crowd. (p87)

Best Live Music

Blue Note Part of a venerable international jazz franchise, with some soul, blues and world music thrown in. (p87)

La Salumeria della Musica This music 'deli' hosts up-and-coming artists alongside big names like Noel Gallagher and Joss Stone. (p112)

☑ Top Tips

▶ Go late and dress to impress; you won't get past the door police if you fail to make *la bella figura*.

▶ Most clubs mix straight and gay. Even at landmark gay/lesbian bars most nights are straight-friendly.

▶ It's no Oxford St, Soho or West Village, but a small dedicated club strip is located in Via Sammartini.

Best
Lake Experiences

Sprinkled with pretty villages, palm trees and dark cypress groves, the Italian lakes have been a favoured holiday destination since the Romans planted their olive trees and built the first holiday villas around their shores. Since then writers, princes, aristrocrats and celebrities have beaten a path to their door, filling the grand Liberty hotels and wandering lakeside promenades.

Best Outdoor Activities

Aero Club Como Flying planes over the lake since 1913, now you can buzz Bellagio in your very own Cessna. (p132)

Lido di Villa Olmo Grab a lounger on the 'beach' or cool off in the world's most scenic public pool. (p132)

Barindelli Boat Tours Make a tour of Lake Como James Bond–style in a mahogany cigarette boat (p129).

Lago Maggiore Express Trace Lake Maggiore's shoreline and cross the 'Hundred Valleys' on this train ride into Switzerland. (p124)

Funicolare Como-Brunate Swing high above the Lake Como in a glass-sided gondola for bird's-eye views. (p132)

Best Lakeside Dining

Taverna del Pittore *Alta cucina* (haute cuisine) on a terrace jutting out over Lake Maggiore. (p123)

Lo Scalo Eat lake perch on Cannobio's pretty cobbled promenade. (p124)

Albergo Silvio Look out over the tiled dome of Santa Maria to the blooming gardens of Villa Carlotta. (p134)

Agriturismo Giacomino Meats, cheeses, honey and wine from the farm accompanied by mountainside views. (p135)

Best Museums

Palazzo Borromeo Set against 10 tiered terraces of blooming flowers, the palace houses Old Masters such as Rubens, Titian and Mantegna. (p118)

Villa Olmo Blockbuster art shows adorn the Liberty-style interiors of Lake Como's grandest neoclassical villa. (p132)

Villa Carlotta Strung with paintings and home to Canova's alabaster sculpture *Cupid and Psyche*. (p133)

Survival Guide

Survival Guide

Before You Go

When to Go

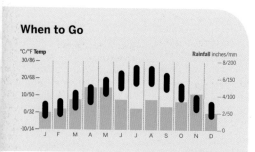

°C/°F Temp
30/86 —
20/68 —
10/50 —
0/32 —
-10/14 —
J F M A M J J A S O N D

Rainfall inches/mm
— 8/200
— 6/150
— 4/100
— 2/50
— 0

➡ **Winter (Nov-Mar)**
The feast of St Ambrose heralds the start of opera season. Epiphany follows with the procession of the Three Kings and February is Carnival.

➡ **Spring (Apr-Jun)**
Furniture Fair turns Milan into a madhouse in April. Escape to blooming lakeside gardens.

➡ **Summer (Jul-Aug)**
Summer is hot, so most Milanese escape the city to lakeside villas or mountain chalets.

➡ **Autumn (Sep-Oct)**
Balmy autumn days see the launch of new exhibitions and spring fashion shows.

Book Your Stay

➡ Milan is an industry to catering to business pro fessionals, which means there's plenty of high-en designer accommodatic and very few bargains.

➡ If you're visiting durin the Furniture Fair or any of the four fashion show you'll need to book at lea a month in advance, if n more.

➡ Some prime hotels are located for easy access to the Fiera, but aren't always convenient for tourists. To be sure, boo somewhere within the second ring road.

➡ Cheaper accommoda tion clusters around the central station and in the Navigli. If staying in the latter watch out for near clubs and book your roo accordingly.

➡ For character, value an a quiet residential vibe seek out hotels in Brera, San Babila and around

Giardini Pubblici and
rso Venezia.

eful Websites

nely Planet (www
elyplanet.com) Book
stels and high-end
tels online.

me Away (www.home
ay.com) Rent apart-
ents and studios direct
m owners for the best
vings in town.

tels in Milan (www
telsinmilan.it) The lead-
g provider for hotel and
&B bookings in Milan.

&B Italia (www.bbitalia.it)
dedicated B&B portal
th prices ranging from
5 to €75 per person.

st Budget

etnamonamour (www
etnamonamour.com) Vi-
ant rooms with a splash
Vietnamese colour.

Cordata (www.ostello
cordata.com) Spotless
ared and private rooms
ecked out with a dash of
esign brio.

tel Casa Mia (www
telcasamia.com) Newly
novated, modern rooms
ose to the Giardini
ubblici.

riston Hotel (www
ristonhotel.com) Kitschy

'70s decor and a fabulous
central location.

Best Midrange

Tara Verde (www.taraverde
.it) A bohemian B&B in a
19th-century palazzo.

Foresteria Monforte
(www.foresteriamonforte.it)
Three classy rooms with
Philippe Starck chairs
and flat-screen TVs.

Hotel Gran Duca di York
(www.ducadiyork.com) Art
Noveau elegance within
a stone's throw of the
Duomo.

Alle Meraviglie (www
.allemeraviglie.it) Six
boutique bedrooms
decorated with Milanese
fabrics and fresh flowers.

**Antica Locanda Leon-
ardo** (www.anticalocanda
leonardo.com) Period furniture and parquet floors in
a 19th-century residence.

Best Top End

Hotel Spadari Duomo
(www.spadarihotel.com)
Rooms at the Spadari are
mini-galleries showcasing
emerging artists.

3Rooms
(www.10corsocomo.com)
Design-styled mansion
suites in the 10 Corso
Como complex.

Hotel STRAF (www.straf.it)
Ultramodern, minimal-
ist rooms with industrial
overtones.

Bulgari Hotel (www
.bulgarihotels.com) Bulgari
elegance in a prime
position behind Brera's
botanic gardens.

Maison Borella (www
.hotelmaisonborella.com)
The only hotel in Milan
overlooking the Navigli
Grande.

**Grand Hotel et de
Milan** (www.grandhotelet
demilan.it) As sumptuous
as it gets with a guest list
including Luchino Vis-
conti and Maria Callas.

Arriving in Milan

Malpensa Airport

Malpensa international
airport (MXP; ☎02 7485
2200; www.sea-aeroporti
milano.it) is 50km north-
west of the city centre.

➡ **Malpensa Express**
(☎800 500005; www
.malpensaexpress.
it) Departs every 30

minutes from Terminal 1 to Stazione Centrale (€10; 52 minutes) and Cadorna's Stazione Nord (€11; 40 minutes) between 6.50am and 9.20pm. Outside these hours there are limited bus services. Passengers arriving or departing from Terminal 2 will need to catch a shuttle bus to the Terminal 1 train station. This is the best option between Malpensa and Milan given the traffic.

➡ **Malpensa Shuttle** (📞02 585 83 185; www .malpensashuttle.it; adult/ reduced €10/5, 45 minutes; ⏱every 20 minutes between 5am and 10.30pm, ticket office 7am-9pm) Runs between the airport and Piazza Luigi di Savoia outside Stazione Centrale, every 20 minutes from 5am to 10.30am, and approximately hourly throughout the rest of the night (€10, 45 minutes).

➡ **Taxi** There is a flat fee of €85 to and from Malpensa to Milan. The drive from Milan should take around 50 minutes outside peak hours. For travellers to Terminal 2, this might prove the quickest option, given poor connections between the two terminals.

Linate Airport

Located 7km east of the city centre, **Linate airport** (📞flight information 02 7485 2200; www.sea-aeroportimi lano.it) handles European and domestic flights.

➡ **Linate Shuttle** (📞02 5858 3185; www .malpensashuttle.it; Piazza Luigi di Savoia; ⏱ticket office 6am-8.30pm Thu-Tue, to 2pm Wed) Runs between the airport and Stazione Centrale every 20 minutes between 6.30am and 11.30pm. Tickets are sold on the bus (€5, 25 minutes).

➡ **Bus 73** (www.atm-mi.it; Piazza San Babila) This city bus departs every 10 to 15 minutes (€1.50, 20 minutes) between 5.30am and 12.30am and stops en route once at Piazza Dateo. Use the normal bus ticket.

Stazione Centrale

International high-speed trains from France and Switzerland arrive in Milan's vast central station (Piazza Duca d'Aosta).

➡ To reach the Piazza di Duomo from here take metro line M3 to Duomo.

➡ To reach the castle take metro line M2 to Cadorna.

➡ To reach Navigli take metro line M2 to Porta Genova.

Getting Around

Milan has an efficient in tegrated public transpo system (www.atm-mi .it) of metro, trams and buses, but when you're moving around the hist ical centre you'll probab find it more convenient to walk. Trams, despite the labyrinthine nature their routes, are actually a good way to see the city while covering more ground.

Bicycle

☑ **Best for...** Touring the historical centre and scooting about Parco Sempione.

➡ **BikeMi** (www.bikemi .it) is Milan's public bike network. Anyone can pic up and drop off bikes at bike stands throughout the city.

➡ Daily, weekly or annua passes are available onlin by phone (📞800 80 81 81) or at ATM info points

Boat

☑ **Best for...** Getting round Lago Maggiore and Lago di Como without the hassle of driving and with better views.

➜ **Navigazione Laghi** (www.navigazionelaghi.it) operates ferries and hydrofoils on the Italian lakes. You can check timetables, prices and book tickets online.

➜ There are ticket booths in each town next to the embarkation quays.

➜ Not all ferries carry cars; check ahead before planning your trip as mistakes mean long drives around the shoreline.

➜ Good value multiday and tourist tickets are available covering a range of tourist sites. Enquire at your nearest ticket booth.

Car & Motorcycle

☑ **Best for...** Out-of-season lake touring, especially around the north of Lago di Como.

➜ It simply isn't worth having a car in Milan. The city is small, easily walkable and parking is nightmare. If you do have a car it's best to leave it in a guarded car park, most of which charge €25 to €40 for 24 hours.

➜ Otherwise street parking costs €1.50 per hour in the centre. To pay buy a SostaMilano card from a tobacconist, scratch off the date and time and display it in your window.

➜ Beware, many streets are pedestrianised or have restricted access.

➜ Having a car to tour the lakes is great out of season, but inadvisable during the summer and holiday weekends, when traffic can slow to a crawl.

➜ Enquire after parking when you book your accommodation, as not all hotels have garage facilities. Even if they do, there is usually a daily fee for parking, typically €10 to €15.

➜ If you're short on time, some ferries carry cars across the lakes between larger towns. Check online for details and prices.

Metro

☑ **Best for...** Quick transport between major sights, connecting to the train station and venturing outside the main tourist areas.

➜ The **metro** (☎800 80 81 81; www.atm-mi.it; ⏱6am-12.30am) has three main underground lines; the red line (MM1) connects the Duomo with Porta Venezia, the castle, Corsa Magenta and the Fiera; the green line (MM2) connects Porta Garibaldi and Brera to Navigli in the south; and the yellow line (MM3) connects the Quad with Porta Romana.

➜ A ticket costs €1.50 and is valid for one metro ride or up to 90 minutes on ATM buses and trams.

➜ Tickets are sold at electronic ticket machines within the stations, or at tobacconists and newspaper stands.

➜ There are various good-value travel passes available. See Tickets & Passes (p163).

Taxi

☑ **Best for...** Arriving at high-end dinner options and the theatre looking as great as you did when you left home; reaching awkward parts of the city and late-night rides back to your hotel.

➜ Taxis are very reliable but expensive at around €10 for the average short trip.

➜ Taxis cannot be flagged down in the street, but must be picked up at designated ranks around the city, usually outside train stations, large hotels and major piazzas.

→ Alternatively you can call for a cab on ☎02 40 40, ☎02 69 69 or ☎02 85 85. English is spoken.

→ Be aware that when you call for a cab, the meter runs from receipt of call, not pick up.

→ There's a fixed rate price for the airports.

Train
☑ **Best for...** Travel to suburban parts of the city and travel to the lakes.

→ The main towns of Stresa and Como on the southern shores of Lake Maggiore and Lake Como, respectively, are served by fast, direct trains from Milan.

→ Stresa is on the Domo-dossola–Milan trainline (€7.40, 75 minutes).

→ Como San Giovanni station is served by trains from Stazione Centrale (€15, 30 minutes).

→ Como's lakeside Stazione FNM (listed on timetables as Como Nord Lago) is served by trains from Cadorna (€3.50, one hour).

Tram & Bus
☑ **Best for...** Scenic rides, connecting to attractions off the metro lines, and for travellers who can't easily walk long distances. A tram ride is also a classic Milanese experience.

→ ATM oversees the metro and trams, along with an extensive bus network.

→ Route maps are available from the ATM Infopoints and at news-stands in the metro stops.

→ Tickets are sold at metro stations, tobacconists and newspaper stands and are valid on buses, trams and metro trains.

→ Tickets must be pre-purchased and validated when boarding.

→ Tickets are good for 90 minutes after validation.

→ Tram 1 is a retro orange beauty with wooden seats and original fittings. It runs along Via Set-tembrini before cutting through the historical centre along Via Manzoni and back towards the Castello Sforzesco.

→ Trams 2 and 3 are also good for sightseeing. Tram 9 loops round the town from Porta Genova to Porta Venezia.

→ For something a bit different, TramATMosfera has been renovated to incorporate a restaurant where you can eat your way through a five-course menu as you tour the city. It departs from Piazza Castello at 1pm and 8pm Tuesday to Sunday. Tickets cost €65.

→ Night services run between 12.30am and 2.30am. There is no service between 2.30am and 6am.

Essential Information
Business Hours
☑ **Top Tip...** Many shops and restaurants close on Monday or are only open from 3pm to 7pm. All civic museums are also closed on Monday. Many smaller shops and restaurants also close for several weeks in August.

Reviews in this guide don't list business hours unless they differ from the following standards:

→ **Banks** 8.30am to 1.30pm and 3.30pm to 4.30pm Monday to Friday

→ **Cafes & bars** 7am to 11pm

→ **Restaurants** noon to 3pm and 7pm to 11pm

uesday to Sunday; some
lso close on Sunday
ight

→ **Shops** 10am to 7pm
uesday to Saturday;
maller shops may also
lose for lunch

→ **Clubs** 10pm to 5am

Electricity

Plugs are standard European two round pins:

→ Voltage 220V

→ Frequency 50Hz

→ Cycle AC

120V/60Hz

Emergency

→ **24-hour pharmacy**
(📞02 669 09 35; Stazione
Centrale, upper gallery)

→ **Ambulance** (📞118)

Tickets & Passes

Milan's public transport system is inexpensive and efficient. Metro, trams and buses all use the same kind of ticket. You can only buy these tickets from metro stations, tobacconists or newsagents – never from the driver. On buses and trams it's the traveller's responsibility to validate their ticket. If you're caught riding without a ticket that's been clearly stamped, you will be fined. For ease of use and to avoid the hassle of validating tickets simply opt for single or multiday passes:

→ **Basic ticket** Valid for 90 minutes; €1.50

→ **One-day ticket** Valid for 24 hours; €4.50

→ **Three-day ticket** Valid for 72 hours; €8.25

→ **Carnet of 10 tickets** Valid for 90 minutes each; €13.80

→ **Luggage ticket** Valid for 1 piece of luggage; €1.50

→ **Carabinieri** (📞112)

→ **English-speaking tourist police** (📞02 86 37 01)

→ **EU-wide emergency hotline** (📞112)

→ **Fire** (📞115)

→ **Municipal Police** (📞02 77 271)

Money
☑ **Top Tip...** ATMs are widely available and are the safest and cheapest way to obtain local currency. However, if you need to change some cash, post offices and banks offer the best rates.

Exchange offices keep longer hours, but watch for higher commissions. To change money you'll need to present your passport as ID.

Currency

→ The euro (€) is Italy's currency. Notes come in denominations of €500, €200, €100, €50, €20, €10 and €5.

Credit cards

→ Visa and MasterCard are among the most widely recognised, but others like Cirrus and

Money-Saving Tips

Milan is Italy's most expensive city and one of the world's top 10. To make the most of your euros consider the following:

➡ Forget taxis – take the Malpensa Express from the airport to the city, then use the metro.

➡ Buy unlimited day passes for the metro, bus and tram.

➡ Buy a SIM card for your phone if you plan on receiving calls or using data.

➡ When it comes to eating don't feel you have to order multiple courses. What were you thinking? That's only for the weekend!

➡ Local trattorie offer the best value meals. Anything with a designer look will come with a designer price tag.

➡ Get into the swing of *aperitivo,* where for the price of a cocktail (€8) you can graze to your heart's content at the buffet bar.

➡ If you book ahead, you can secure the cheaper seats at La Scala (€25 to €40).

➡ Some of Milan's best experiences are free: the Duomo, window-shopping in the Quadrilatero d'Oro, picnicking in Parco Sempione, riding Tram 1 and eating gelati in front of San Lorenzo.

Maestro are also well covered. American Express and Diners Club are not universally accepted, so check in advance.

Tipping

➡ If service isn't included on the bill, leave a 10% to 15% tip. If it is, leave a little extra for good service. In bars, most Italians just leave small change (€0.10 to €0.20 is fine). Tipping taxi drivers isn't normal practice, but you should tip porters and staff at high-end hotels.

Public Holidays

☑ **Top Tip...** If you're in town over Easter remember to stock up the fridge or reserve a table for a slap-up lunch on Easter Sunday.

Banks, offices, and some shops will be closed on public holidays. Restaurants, museums and tourist attractions tend to stay open.

➡ **New Year's Day** 1 January

➡ **Epiphany** 6 January

➡ **Easter Monday** March/April

➡ **Liberation Day** 25 Apr

➡ **Labour Day** 1 May

➡ **Republic Day** 2 June

➡ **Feast of the Assumption** 15 August

➡ **All Saints Day** 1 November

➡ **Festa di Sant'Ambrogio** 7 December

➡ **Feast of the Immaculate Conception** 8 December

➡ **Christmas Day** 25 December

➡ **Festa di San Stefano** 26 December

Safe Travel

Milan is a safe and affluent destination, although like any major city pickpocketing can be an issue at busy train stations and the Piazza di Duomo. If you're the victim of theft or crime, simply find the nearest police station and report the incident. For insurance purposes you'll need to fill in any relevant forms. For lost or stolen passports contact your embassy.

Telephone

☑ **Top Tip...** If you need to make cheap calls, or if you want to have a number where you can be easily reached, buy an Italian SIM card and pop it into your phone. You can buy them, and activate the number, at any mobile-phone service shop.

➜ Italy uses GSM 900/1800, which is compatible with the rest of Europe and Australia but not with North American GSM 1900 or the Japanese system.

Mobile Phones

➜ To buy a SIM card you'll need to supply your passport and the address of your accommodation.

➜ The main mobile phone providers are TIM (Telecom Italia Mobile), Wind and Vodafone.

Country & City Codes

➜ The dialling code for Italy is 39. The city code for Milan is 02, which precedes local numbers. The city code is an integral part of the number and must always be dialled.

➜ Mobile phone numbers begin with a three-digit prefix such as 330.

➜ Toll-free (free-phone) numbers are known as *numeri verdi* and usually start with 800.

Useful Phone Numbers

➜ For local directory inquiries dial ☎12.

➜ See also Emergency (p163)

Tourist Information

Central tourist office (Map p74, D5; ☎02 7740 4343; www.provincia.milano .it/turismo; Piazza

Castello 1; ⏰9am-6pm Mon-Fri, 9am-1.30pm & 2-6pm Sat, 9am-1pm & 2-5pm Sun; Ⓜ Cairoli) has a huge supply of maps, brochures and tours. The office maintains listings of hotels, but there's no booking facility. **Welcome Desk Meeting Milan** has offices at **Linate** (☎02 702 00 443; Linate Airport; ⏰7.30am-11.30pm) and **Malpensa** (☎02 5858 0080; Terminal 1, Malpensa Airport; ⏰8am-8pm) airports, as well as the Stazione Centrale.

Travellers with Disabilities

Milan is not an easy destination for travellers with a disability. But for those with limited mobility, ATM has recently introduced low-floor buses on many of its routes and some metro stations are equipped with lifts. See the dual-language **Milano Per Tutti** (www. milanopertutti.it) for details as well as itineraries of accessible sights.

Language

Standard Italian is taught and spoken throughout Italy. Regional dialects are an important part of identity in many parts of the country, but you'll have no trouble being understood anywhere if you stick to standard Italian, which we've also used in this chapter.

The sounds used in spoken Italian can all be found in English. If you read our pronunciation guides as if they were English, you'll be understood. The stressed syllables are indicated with italics. Note that *ai* is pronounced as in 'aisle', *ay* as in 'say', *ow* as in 'how', *dz* as the 'ds' in 'lids', and that *r* is a strong and rolled sound.

To enhance your trip with a phrasebook, visit **lonelyplanet.com**. Lonely Planet iPhone phrasebooks are available through the Apple App store.

Basics

Hello.
Buongiorno.   bwon·*jor*·no

Goodbye.
Arrivederci.   a·ree·ve·*der*·chee

How are you?
Come sta?   *ko*·me sta

Fine. And you?
Bene. E Lei?   *be*·ne e lay

Please.
Per favore.   per fa·*vo*·re

Thank you.
Grazie.   *gra*·tsye

Excuse me.
Mi scusi.   mee *skoo*·zee

Sorry.
Mi dispiace.   mee dees·*pya*·che

Yes./No.
Sì./No.   see/no

I don't understand.
Non capisco.   non ka·*pee*·sko

Do you speak English?
Parla inglese?   *par*·la een·*gle*·ze

Eating & Drinking

I'd like ...   *Vorrei ...*   vo·*ray* ..

a coffee   *un caffè*   oon ka·*fe*

a table   *un tavolo*   oon *ta*·vo·lo

the menu   *il menù*   eel me·*noo*

two beers   *due birre*   *doo*·e *bee*·re

What would you recommend?
Cosa mi   *ko*·za mee
consiglia?   kon·*see*·lya

Enjoy the meal!
Buon appetito!   bwon a·pe·*tee*·to

That was delicious!
Era squisito!   *e*·ra skwee·*zee*·to

Cheers!
Salute!   sa·*loo*·te

Please bring the bill.
Mi porta il conto,   mee *por*·ta eel *kon*·to
per favore?   per fa·*vo*·re

Shopping

I'd like to buy ...
Vorrei comprare ...   vo·*ray* kom·*pra*·re

I'm just looking.
Sto solo   sto *so*·lo
guardando.   gwar·*dan*·do

How much is this?

Quanto costa questo?	kwan·to kos·ta kwe·sto

It's too expensive.

È troppo caro/ cara. (m/f) | e tro·po ka·ro/ ka·ra

Emergencies

Help!

Aiuto! | a·yoo·to

Call the police!

Chiami la polizia! | kya·mee la po·lee·tsee·a

Call a doctor!

Chiami un medico! | kya·mee oon me·dee·ko

I'm sick.

Mi sento male. | mee sen·to ma·le

I'm lost.

Mi sono perso/ persa. (m/f) | mee so·no per·so/ per·sa

Where are the toilets?

Dove sono i gabinetti? | do·ve so·no ee ga·bee·ne·tee

Time & Numbers

What time is it?

Che ora è? | ke o·ra e

It's (two) o'clock.

Sono le (due). | so·no le (doo·e)

morning	mattina	ma·tee·na
afternoon	pomeriggio	po·me·ree·jo
evening	sera	se·ra
yesterday	ieri	ye·ree
today	oggi	o·jee
tomorrow	domani	do·ma·nee

1	uno	oo·no
2	due	doo·e
3	tre	tre
4	quattro	kwa·tro
5	cinque	cheen·kwe
6	sei	say
7	sette	se·te
8	otto	o·to
9	nove	no·ve
10	dieci	dye·chee
100	cento	chen·to
1000	mille	mee·le

Transport & Directions

Where's ...?

Dov'è ...? | do·ve ...

What's the address?

Qual è l'indirizzo? | kwa·le leen·dee·ree·tso

Can you show me (on the map)?

Può mostrarmi (sulla pianta)? | pwo mos·trar·mee (soo·la pyan·ta)

At what time does the ... leave?

A che ora parte ...? | a ke o·ra par·te ...

Does it stop at ...?

Si ferma a ...? | see fer·ma a ...

How do I get there?

Come ci si arriva? | ko·me chee see a·ree·va

bus	l'autobus	low·to·boos
ticket	un biglietto	oon bee·lye·to
timetable	orario	o·ra·ryo
train	il treno	eel tre·no

Index

See also separate subindexes for:

🗙 **Eating p173**

🍸 **Drinking p173**

✪ **Entertainment p174**

🔒 **Shopping p174**

Sights p000
Map Pages p000

Behind the Scenes

Send Us Your Feedback

We love to hear from travellers – your comments help make our books better. We read every word, and we guarantee that your feedback goes straight to the authors. Visit **lonelyplanet.com/contact** to submit your updates and suggestions.

Note: We may edit, reproduce and incorporate your comments in Lonely Planet products such as guidebooks, websites and digital products, so let us know if you don't want your comments reproduced or your name acknowledged. For a copy of our privacy policy visit lonelyplanet.com/privacy.

Our Readers

Many thanks to the travellers who used the last edition and wrote to us with helpful hints, useful advice and interesting anecdotes:

Gianluca Mammone, Sarah Pollini, Stefania Vele

Paula Hardy's Thanks

Doors opened in Milan and beyond because of the generosity of Claudio and Paola Bonacina, Paola Cairo, Angelo Proietti, Isabella Albertazzi, Dario Monti, Marco Roverso, Emanuele Ficchì, Deborah Favaron, Sabrina Landini and Giovanni at Foresteria Monforte. Last but never least, thank you to Rob for being such a gallant gourmet.

Acknowledgments

Cover photograph: On the roof of Milan's Duomo; Hauke Dressier/Getty Images ©.

This Book

This 2nd edition of Lonely Planet's *Pocket Milan & The Lakes* guidebook was researched and written by Paula Hardy. The previous edition was written by Donna Wheeler. This book was commissioned in Lonely Planet's London office, and produced by the following:

Commissioning Editor Joe Bindloss **Coordinating Editors** Pete Cruttenden, Justin Flynn **Coordinating Cartographer** Samantha Tyson **Coordinating Layout Designer** Sandra Helou **Senior Editor** Andi Jones **Managing Editors** Anna Metcalfe, Annelies Mertens **Managing Cartographers** Anita Banh, Anthony Phelan **Managing Layout Designer** Chris Girdler **Cover Research** Naomi Parker

Internal Image Research Aude Vauconsant **Language Content** Samantha Forge **Thanks to** Dan Austin, Ryan Evans, Jouve India, Asha Ioculari, Sophie Marozeau, Mardi O'Connor, Trent Paton, Martine Power, Joe Revill, Raphael Richards, Averil Robertson, Wibowo Rusli, Amanda Sierp, Fiona Siseman, Andrew Stapleton, Gerard Walker, Danny Williams

Our Writer

Paula Hardy

Paula has been contributing to Lonely Planet's Italian guides for over a decade. She has worked on five editions of the *Italy* guide, coordinated the 1st edition of *Puglia & Basilicata* and has written several editions of both *Sicily* and *Sardinia*. Slowly working her way up Lo Stivalo (the Boot), Paula's first experience of Milan and the Lakes was Furniture Fair madness, bravely swimming in frigid waters and toting a suitcase full of impractical shoes. These days she knows better and focuses on the dynamic art scene, iconic designers and Heidi-like mountain walking. An erstwhile editor and producer, she also contributes to and edits a variety of websites and travel publications. You can find her tweeting @paula6hardy.

Published by Lonely Planet Publications Pty Ltd
ABN 36 005 607 983
2nd edition – Jan 2013
ISBN 978 1 74179 779 4
© Lonely Planet 2013   Photographs © as indicated 2013
10 9 8 7 6 5 4 3 2 1
Printed in China